Philosophy

A Crash Course to History's Great Thinkers

By Paxton Casmiro

Philosophy : A Crash Course Copyright © 2016 by Paxton Casmiro.

ISBN: 978-1535311786

First Edition: July 2016

978-1535311786

CONTENTS

INTRODUCTION

Philosophy answers the basic questions of life. However, because the language and vocabulary used is difficult to understand, many people avoid the subject. This book attempts to make philosophy easier to understand and interesting. It also discusses the philosophical contributions of many modern, contemporary philosophers.

PART 1: WHAT IS PHILOSOPHY?

Philosophy is a social science that explores the fundamental questions of life. It seeks to answer the following:

- Who am I?
- Why am I here?
- What is truth?
- What is reality?
- What is beauty?
- What should I do and not do?
- Who is God?

These are just a few of the questions that philosophers have attempted to answer throughout the ages. Their answers differ, and one must choose what to believe. However, reading about answers philosophers have written about will definitely make one think and come closer to the "right" answer for himself or herself. Each person can develop his or her own philosophy of life from reading in the discipline of philosophy. Philosophers often think that they are creating an accurate model with which to understand life, but the explanations reflect bias and personal views that come from experiences of the philosopher. Since philosophers are imperfect, they often disagree with one another.

Philosophy is translated from the Greek words *philio*, which means love, and *sophis*, meaning wisdom. So philosophy literally means "a love of wisdom." It is a discipline that attempts to get at the truth of life. It can give one a framework for thinking about life. It attempts to present the big picture of life in an organized fashion. Philosophy attempts to tell how people think, how we are present, how we act and should act, and how we see the world.

Philosophy has many branches. Metaphysics studies the universe and reality. Logic explains how to create a valid argument. Epistemology examines knowledge and how one knows. Political philosophy studies the rights of people and the roles of government in people's lives. Ethics is the study of morality and how one should live.

Perhaps a good plan for reading this book is for you to answer the questions above and the questions below, also found at the beginning of the chapters. After reading the book, see if your answers have changed. You may be more confused about your answers, or you may be more decisive after reading the thoughts of the great minds of history. In any event, enjoy your journey!

PART 2: PHILOSOPHERS

Timeline:

When attempting to understand philosophy, it is helpful to know in what time period certain philosophers and philosophies were prevalent. Frequently, the philosophy reflects the social, economic, and political events of the time. Philosophers are affected by philosophers that they have studies and what they believe or refute from previous philosophies. Therefore, understanding when the philosopher lived and when the philosophy was prevalent helps to get the big picture of philosophy clearer. The date given is the philosopher's birth year. Following the name is the school of thought that philosopher is associated with or the historical movement.

- 106 BC- Cicero- Roman
- 569 BC- Pythagoras- Greek
- 551 BC- Confucius- Chinese
- 470 BC- Socrates- Greek
- 428 BC- Plato- Greek
- 384 BC- Aristotle- Greek
- 341 BC- Epicurus- Roman
- 4 BC- Seneca- Roman
- 25 CE- Laozi- Chinese
- 1225 CE- St. Thomas Aquinas- Medieval
- 1400 CE- Ockham- Medieval
- 1469 CE- Machiavelli- Renaissance
- 1561 CE- Francis Bacon- Enlightenment

- 1596 CE- Descartes-Enlightenment
- 1632 CE- John Locke-Enlightenment
- 1646 CE- Leibniz-Enlightenment
- 1711 CE- Hume-Enlightenment
- 1712 CE-Rousseau-Enlightenment
- 1724 CE- Kant-Enlightenment
- 1770 CE- Hegel- Post-Enlightenment
- 1806 CE- Mill-Utilitarianism
- 1813 CE- Kierkegaard-Romanticism
- 1818 CE- Karl Marx-Materialism
- 1842 CE- William James-American
- 1844 CE- Nietzsche-Nihilism
- 1889 CE- Heidegger- Pre-existentialist
- 1905 CE- Sartre-Existentialism
- 1906 CE- Hannah Arendt- Political theorist
- 1910 CE- A. J. Ayer - Positivism
- 1911 CE- Marshall McLuhan- Post Modernism
- 1917 CE- David Bohm- Post

Modernism

- 1919 CE- Iris Murdoch- Post Modernism
- 1922 CE- Thomas Kuhn- Post Modernism
- 1926 CE- Michael Foucault- Post Modernism
- 1929 CE- Jean Baudrillard- Post Modernism
- 1929 CE- Harry Frankfurt- Post Modernism
- 1967 CE- Sam Harris- Post Modernism
- 1968 CE- Julian Baggini- Post Modernism

CHAPTER 1: CICERO

For what, in the name of heaven, is more to be desired than wisdom? What more to be prized? What is better for a man, what more worthy of his nature?

For what, in the name of heaven, is more to be desired than wisdom? What more to be prized? What is better for a man, what more worthy of his nature?

How should one choose a career?

Marcus Tullius Cicero was born of a wealthy, but not aristocratic landowning family. He and his brother Quintus were given a top education, and they were expected to impact their world in a great way by their father. Cicero became an assistant to generals, but he did not like war, so he became a lawyer. He desired to learn Greek philosophy and law, so he traveled and learned from Epicureans of the day. Returning to Rome, he moved up in government until he was appointed consul.

Cicero defended philosophy as more important than material success. He credits philosophy with providing the answers to social and moral dilemmas. He believed the universe was run by a divine plan and that each person was a spark from God. Since we were all part of God, doing wrong to another was doing wrong to ourselves. Denial of a responsibility to our fellowman because we do not know him intimately is society's ruin, according to Cicero. He says man is a social creature, and the goal of life should be to help one another by kind acts. He says our responsibility should be first to our parents and country, then to our children and family, and finally to other citizens. We should always do what is right, and we will benefit from that action. Performing even a small act that is wrong will multiply into that major consequences. We are to resist arrogance and pride.

Cicero advocates self-control and believes man should practice simplicity and self-denial. We should use our gifts and do what is right for us, choosing a career and lifestyle that matches our character.

CHAPTER 2: PYTHAGORAS

The Pythagorean ... having been brought up in the study of mathematics, thought that things are numbers ... and that the whole cosmos is a scale and a number. –Aristotle

How important is mathematics to an understanding of the world?

Pythagoras is referred to as the first mathematician. He was also a philosopher, although we have none of his writings, only reports from his contemporaries and students. They describe him as a divine, god-like figure. He led a religious scientific circle which followed a code of secrecy. This circle of thinkers discussed questions about what a good life was like, what justice was, and other philosophical questions. The group was called the "matematikoi", and they were mandated to keep secret their discussions and activities. Loyalty to the group was demanded of all members. They were not allowed to have any material possessions at all.

Pythagoras' father was a merchant who came from Tyre, and there is a legend that Pythagoras traveled with his father, and was taught by the Chaldeans and the wise men from Syria. Later Pythagoras went to Egypt, where he visited temples and learned from priests there. He adopted some of the Egyptian priests' characteristics, specifically his refusal to wear clothes made from animal skins and refusal to eat beans. He was a vegetarian as well. Like the priests, he strove for purity in life. He learned from the Babylonians when he was there as a prisoner of war later in life.

Pythagoras philosophy states that reality is mathematics, and some numbers have a mystical significance. He believed that thinking can bring spiritual purification and bring the soul in union with the divine. Pythagoreans talked about cosmical harmony, which is based on numbers as the relations of things. For example, they discovered that halving the length of a string on a lyre made the note one octave higher, and that all harmonies represent ratios of whole numbers. He extended the concept of harmony into everything, and discussed the harmony of the spheres of the universe.

Pythagoras also was one of the first to develop a system for deductive reasoning. He started with a statement that is self-evident, and proceeded step by step logically to a conclusion that is not self-evident.

Pythagoras studied properties of numbers, and developed the concept and properties of even and odd numbers, triangular numbers, perfect numbers, geometry proofs, and Pythagoras's theorem. He observed, and proved, that the angles of a triangle equaled two right angles. He also proved that the square of the legs of a right triangle is equal to the hypotenuse, the other part of the triangle. (A squared plus B squared equals C squared.) He also believed that the dodecahedron embodied the entire universe.

Pythagoras also taught that the Earth was a sphere at the center of the Universe. He also stated that Venus was a planet and not a star.

Ethical tenets of Pythagoras and his followers were that the most important things are friendship, unselfishness, and honesty.

CHAPTER 3:
CONFUCIUS

"The superior man thinks of virtue; the small man thinks of comfort…. Virtue is gravity, generosity of soul, sincerity, earnestness, and kindness."

How important is tradition and loyalty to family?

The philosophies and ethics of Confucius reigned in China for hundreds of years until changed by Chairman Mao's

Cultural Revolution. The country appears to be returning to some of Confucius' ideas with its teaching of Confucius being incorporated into education. Confucius believed in the importance of family and loyalty to family as one of the most important characteristics of a virtuous man. He taught that caring for one's parents is required when one becomes old enough to do so. He was a proponent of public service for all, and selflessness is critical to happiness. Confucius believed in tradition and following the rules of propriety. Instead of changing to fit an evolving society, Confucius believed that people should follow the rules of life that have existed for centuries.

Harmony in relationships with family and friends is necessary for a good life. While differences are to be respected, all people are to work together for the common good. Benevolence is a trait that must be developed, and respect for others is required at all times.

A wise person always does what is right, and he is virtuous. Without virtue, there is chaos. A wise person will continue to learn throughout his life, according to Confucius. Learning the power of words will help one to know others and to know life.

Confucius created the idea of the Golden Rule: do to others as you would have them do to you. He is also credited with the development of yin and yang, those two forces that are constantly in conflict and thereby create change and contradiction. To achieve fulfillment, one must reconcile the opposites and settle in the middle.

Confucius' view of government was that it is created to make life better for its citizens. Rather than develop punishments for those who break laws, the government must create policies that lead people toward virtue. Life is better when people want to do good, rather than just fear being caught for doing wrong. Leaders should not be influenced by the wealthy, dishonest citizens, but they should set an example for the people and advance those who are morally good. Leaders should make sure people are paid well and rewarded for their work. Patience is required when leading people, and rash change is not good for the country. Reliance on tradition and past leaders' wisdom is the key to success.

Little is known of Confucius' life. He was from the area of China now known as Shandong province, and was believed to be a descendant of the Shang Dynasty. His father died when he was very young, so he was poor. He worked many jobs, but his wisdom attracted followers, about 3000. He became one who trained young men for service.

CHAPTER 4:
SOCRATES

"An unexamined life is not worth living."
Do you know yourself well?

Socrates: Life and philosophy

Socrates developed a philosophy based on the question, "What makes a good life?" This question is one of the basic questions of life. People want to know how to be happy and live well. In his evaluation of this question, Socrates answered questions about morality, social norms, and politics. His conclusions were written down by his students and contemporaries, and the texts of others are what we know about Socrates.

Socrates was a poor stone mason, and he had only a basic Greek education. He served in the military during the Peloponnesian War, and served in three military campaigns. He was known for his bravery and fearlessness. He dressed in rags and went barefoot. He had three sons by a much younger wife, Xanthippe. He was vocal about his political views, which went against the views of those in power. He was arrested and brought to trial for his anti-religious views and for corrupting the youth of the city. He was found to be guilty, and he had a choice: he could go into exile or he could drink poison hemlock. Still fearless, he drank the poison down and died.

Socrates believed that self-examination

was critical for true wisdom. He believed that a person's actions were based on his intelligence. A person should develop wisdom and self-knowledge, rather than material objects or wealth. He saw himself as a gad-fly, stirring up the lazy. He did not lecture and espouse his views publically, but went about the city asking questions of all people that he encountered. He stated that all men were his teachers, and he was very social. His method of questioning is one of his best known legacies, and the Socratic method is still used in many classrooms today. The method known as the Socratic method is called the "elenchus." In this method of questioning, a debate format was used. An individual made a statement to Socrates, perhaps in response to a question. Socrates would give an example of an instance in which the answer given would not be true. He played "Devil's advocate." This response would lead to more questions and more scenarios to refute the prior claim. Socrates would switch sides in the debate frequently to keep the individual thinking and evaluating his thinking.

Socrates described a new type of ethical behavior for his time. Rather than being a proponent of the sophism that was prevalent during his time, he was the biggest challenger to sophism, which focuses on man rather than the divine. Socrates based his ethical values on logical reasoning, rather than theological beliefs, which ultimately led to his death. He did not deny truth exists, but he says it can only be found through hard work.

His view about death was that the guardian spirit who had been given to us at birth proceeds to lead us to a certain place at the moment of death.

Chapter 5: Plato

"Until kings are philosophers or philosophers are kings, cities will never cease from ill."

What makes up one's soul?

Who should run a nation?

      Plato wrote many works in his lifetime, not texts, but lively discussions that were similar to mysteries, with the truth the "hunted criminal." Much of Plato's written work consists of ideas that he learned from Socrates. Plato addresses many of the big questions of life in his works. Like Socrates,

Plato teaches his philosophy by questioning and refuting arguments, the Socratic method. Therefore, he encourages people to decide for themselves what the answers are to life's questions. He impels people to think and rethink about these important questions, but he never answers them himself.

Plato begins his writing questioning the meaning and importance of justice. He states that Socrates believed that a life without well-meaning actions, justice, is worthless. Justice is not optional, but it is the foundation of life and relationships.

Plato defines reality with his theory of forms. He states that reality is actually what one sees and hears and also one's thoughts about the visible world. One's thoughts are unaffected by changes in the world, and concepts that are abstract like beauty, justice, and courage are just as important as what one learns through the senses.

The human soul is made up of three parts, according to Plato. The three parts, reason, spirit, and appetite, are constantly at war with each other to rule the person. Reason is the part responsible for thinking and understanding, leading to rational decision. Spirit is the part of the soul seeking victory and honor, and if not attained, will lead one to anger, shame, and bitterness. Appetite is the seat of one's desires and basic cravings, such as hunger, thirst, and sexual desires. The individual who is just, fulfilled in life, will allow reason to control the spirit and the appetite. Reason will be influenced by Good, and will provide balance and satisfaction for a balanced life. Education should be centered around knowing the Good and seeking wisdom, and negativity and immorality should never be included in learning.

Justification for the belief that the mind is separate from the body, dualism, was the self-evident fact that the mind can exist before the body and after the body is no longer alive; therefore, this is evidence that they are separate parts. He stated that endings are always beginnings, so death is a new beginning. Similarly, he states that the new always replaces the old, so it must be true in life and death as well.

Plato espoused ideas that were well before his time, including the equality of women and social engineering. He stated that women should be given the same opportunities for education and work as men, and they should have the opportunity to rule if qualified. He believed marriages should be arranged so as to produce the best children for the state. He felt that children should be educated to benefit the state, and children should be raised in state nurseries, leaving the parents to work and contribute to society.

Plato's views of government were nontraditional as well. He did not support direct democracy, tyranny, or oligarchy, but instead felt that the government should be made up of a group of philosophers who were to work for the good of the state. They were to abandon their life of contemplation, and use their wisdom and intelligence to make decisions for the nation. He believed the quality of the men would outweigh their lack of experience in ruling and administration. He believed citizens were of three classes: elite guardians, soldiers, and the masses. He felt training the elite was very important. He compared the guardians to reason, soldiers to courage, and the masses of people as the appetite, or desire of a man.

One illustration Plato makes in *The*

Republic, his treatise, is an allegory called the allegory of the cave. In this anecdote, a group of prisoners are chained together in a cave so that they cannot move and can only see what is in front of them, a stone wall. They have been in this place since birth. Behind and above them is a fire. Between the fire and the people, other people walk while carrying things on their heads. The only thing they have ever seen is the shadow on the wall. They think the shadows are reality. If someone holds a book behind them, they think that they have seen a book. If someone showed them an actual book, they would not recognize it because it would not what they had learned was a book, but was, in fact, the shadow of a book. The illusion of a book is more real to the prisoners than the book itself. If a prisoner were forced to go outside into the light, he would be upset by this strange world and blinded by the light.

Eventually the prisoner would adjust to the light and realize the reality he knew in the cave was not reality. Now if the prisoner went back into the cave to free the other prisoners and told them what he knew now about illusion and reality, they would not believe him. They threaten to kill him if he sets them free. The illusion that they believe is real and that they are familiar with is preferable to something they do not know or believe. Plato asserts that mankind is like the prisoners in the cave. If they are confronted with a truth that they are not familiar with, they will be frightened and want to turn back to the familiar, but unreal illusion. He summarizes this truth with the assertion that knowledge learned through the senses is just perception and opinion and not real truth. He believed that the only truth was that discovered by philosophical reasoning, not one's senses.

Plato addressed the issue of ethics with his anecdote of the ring that one could put on and make him invisible. He asked one to reflect on what he would do with such a ring. Would he behave the same or differently? What would he do differently? The answers to those questions are a test of ethical behavior or character. Plato believed that there are eternal truths known only through pure reason, and that these reason sees through perceptions of the senses and illusions to discover the absolute and unchangeable truth.

Plato felt that artists should not be allowed to create their art any way that they wanted, but that they have a moral, as well as aesthetic, responsibility. This social responsibility is a realization of the impact that artists have on those who are the audience for the play or tale or painting. Teaching morals and influencing youth is just as important as aesthetics in art.

Plato was born in Athens into the aristocratic class, so he was taught by the best thinkers in Greece. Socrates was his mentor, and he left Athens when Socrates was killed. Much we know of Socrates comes from Aristotle. While he likely would have gone into politics without the influence of Socrates, he instead founded a school where he and other philosophers taught philosophy and mathematics when he returned to Athens.

Plato's school was a model for all universities. It had scientific equipment and a library, and its goal was to train men to think for themselves. The education was a joint effort between teacher and pupil, a dialectic process. His theory of education refers to "anamnesis", the idea that knowledge is remembering. He believed the soul or mind passed through many states, and the knowledge learned in this cycle of being needs to be awakened. Plato saw himself as a midwife, bringing this knowledge out into the world.

CHAPTER 6:
ARISTOTLE

We are what we repeatedly do. Excellence,
then, is not an act, but a habit.

How do you find happiness in life?

Aristotle was a student of Plato's for 20 years, but his conclusions about life were very different from those of his master teacher. His mentor provoked him to thought, but his conclusions are almost totally opposite from those of Plato. While Plato believed that truth could not be discovered through the senses, but by thought, Aristotle believed that truth could be learned only through the senses. He was the model scientist, unbiased and impersonal. He believed that life lived according to reason is a divine life that enables one to rise to the immortal. Reason gives man everything, and epitomizes "the Greek way."

Aristotle believed that to understand the reality of objects, one would have to understand the function of the object. For example, a car is just a hunk of metal until one understands that it takes one from one place to another. It is function that makes an object what it really is.

What then is the function of a human being? Aristotle says that seeing, smelling, or moving are not the function of a human being because those things can be done by a horse or a dog. The difference between humans and all other things is the ability to act according to reason, something only humans can do. Only humans can organize their thoughts and their lives, so that makes them unique.

Aristotle believed that a person is a sum of the virtues that he has cultivated in his life, and his virtues come from the choices he has made. One is great when he has organized his life according to the highest virtues. He rejected Plato's ideas about art having to combine the moral with the aesthetic, and he said that it is inappropriate to demand ethics be part of art. He believed that esthics is just a guide to living the good life.

Aristotle believed that God is a God of reason. He is self-sufficient, unchanging, and omniscient. He has no need to discover any truth because He knows everything already. He is perfect .He is wise. Therefore, Aristotle had little patience with the notions of the Greek gods like Zeus, Diana, and Triton; they lied and plotted, and were far from imperfect.

Happiness is equivalent to success, according to Aristotle. Rational people will organize their life so that they can flourish and achieve the ultimate good. If one pursues only pleasure, he will be deprived of meaningful, purposeful activity, so he will not be happy. Aristotle compared people who only seek immediate gratification to "grazing animals", who never move forward. To have a good life, one must combine work with virtue, constantly learning and improving oneself. Virtue involves choice, and the correct choice was referred to as the "mean". Human life is the search for happiness, which is the search for an activity or process through which one can bring fulfillment to self and others. Helping others to flourish is tied to excellence. The important task of life is learning who you are, and developing the talents you have, and then putting them to work to benefit others. Learning is one of the greatest joys in life, because one never completes the task, learning all there is to know.

Friendship is good because it allows people to think and reason together and work together to meet their goals.

Aristotle believed that reality is made up of the intelligible world, thoughts and ideas; the sense world, observed through the senses; and both worlds are necessary. Separating the two would be impossible and accomplish nothing.

There are four ways things come into being, according to Aristotle. There is the material, that involves what things are made of; the formal, that describes the form that they take; the efficient, which describes the process by which something comes into being; and the final cause, the purpose of the thing.

He explained change by using the ideas of actuality and potentiality. The substance is the bearer of qualities, but something needs to be added for the potential to occur. He focused on becoming rather than being.

Aristotle's view of politics was that political stability could be achieved with a strong middle class to create a mean between tyranny and democracy. He did feel women were unfit for freedom.

Logic is also believed to be developed by Aristotle, and this form of logic is still used today. Aristotle described logic as a tool for reasoning and thinking. He developed the syllogism, a method for deductive reasoning, which consists of two premises followed by a conclusion. He then made up rules for the logic syllogisms.

One premise has to be universal, that is that it includes the word "all". One premise has to be affirmative, that is it makes a statement. If a premise is positive, then the conclusion will be a positive one. If one of the premises is negative, then the conclusion will be negative. An example of a positive syllogism follows:

Premise 1: Dogs are animals.

Premise 2: All animals die.

Conclusion: Therefore, all dogs die.

An example of a negative syllogism follows:

Premise 1: Oaks are trees.

Premise 2: All trees cannot live without healthy roots.

Conclusion: Therefore, oaks cannot live without healthy roots.

The formula for syllogisms is " All A are B, and all B are C, then all A are C."

Aristotle also stated other rules that apply to all thinking. One of these is the law of identity. It states that all things have characteristics that make them what they are. For example, a cat is a cat because it has fur, claws, and it purrs. That's what makes it a cat.

Another law is the law of noncontradiction. This law states that something cannot be true and false at the same time. For example, a cat cannot be a cat and not a cat at the same time.

A third law is the law of the excluded middle. This law states that a statement can be either true or false, and there is no middle ground. If you say Bucky is a dog, then it must be true or false; there is no other option.

Aristotle was born in Macedonia in what is now Northern Greece. His father was a doctor to the king. He studied under the great thinkers of the time. When his teacher, Plato, died, he traveled and studied under other scholars. He also did research in areas that are now called biology, geography, and botany. He was one of the first to subdivide areas of knowledge, creating a classification system of learning. He refers to over 500 different species of animals, and classified life forms. He said that we need to study what we observe, rather than theorizing about what is unknown.

He studied language itself and the features of language. He came up with ten features of speech. They are substance, quality, quantity, relation, place, time, position, state, action, and affection. Much of his work is lost, but there is still a massive amount of his writing that contains ground breaking thoughts for all times. He believed poetry was more important than history because it deals with universals. His writing is not as entertaining as that of Plato, and is referred to as the "boring professor" at times.

CHAPTER 7: EPICURUS

Every pleasure, therefore, because of its natural relationship to us, is good, but not every pleasure is to be chosen.

Does indulging in pleasure bring happiness?

While many think of gourmet food when they think of Epicurus, his philosophical outlook was much more than that. He believed that living simply, with reason, is the key to happiness. He believed that once basic needs have been met, and one enjoys friends and the world around him, he is happy.

He believed that what is real is what we can learn from our senses. He did not believe in an afterlife, so what we do here on earth is what really matters, and enjoying life is most important. He discussed death and said that it is no concern of ours and we should not fear it. He says that while we are alive, we are not dead, and it is irrational to fear what is not reality. He says that at any given time, we exist or death exists, so it would be irrational to fear something that does not currently exist.

The origins of the universe were part of philosophy at the time Epicurus lived, so he has left his view of the universe in the papyrus scrolls that he wrote. He believes that knowing the universe can come from our observations, and stories and myths should not be believed. Rather than believing the gods caused weather or earthquakes, for example, Epicurus believed conditions in the atmosphere or the physical world caused these phenomena. He did not believe in luck or chance, and he advised men not to pursue choices dependent on luck.

Epicurus believed that the world had always been, and was not created by God. He believed that man's troubles come from attempting to subvert the laws of the universe. He believed one should learn as much as he can reduce fear and superstition. He believed seeking serenity and calmness is the best actions that we can take. Avoiding pain and mental anguish is the goal of life.

Epicurus' discourse on ethics suggested finding a good man, keeping our sights on him, live as if he were watching us, and do everything as if he sees what we are doing.

Food was discussed in Epicurus' philosophy, and his view of food was to enjoy gourmet food only occasionally to really appreciate it, and simple food is best on a daily basis.

Epicurus was born in Greece, and he learned at the feet of a student of Plato. He began a school in Athens, and he admitted women and slaves into his school. While legend implies that sensuality is a primary goal of man, this legend was perpetuated by Christianity, and it is not accurate. He was a man who taught simple enjoyment of life and friends was the key to happiness.

CHAPTER 8. SENECA

If one does not know to which port one is sailing, no wind is preferable.

Is attitude as or more important than action?

Seneca was from Rome, rather than from Greece as were many early philosophers. He was Emperor Nero's tutor, and, therefore, was a political advisor to him when he began to reign in Rome. He was the real master of the world for ten years. Unfortunately, the political intrigue of the time was deadly to him. He asked to retire from service to Nero, but was denied the right to retire. Shortly after, he was accused of being part of a plot to assassinate Nero, and was forced to commit suicide.

Seneca is representative of Stoicism, a school of thought in philosophical theory. In his writings, he depicts a person who is seeking relief from distress of the soul, and he writes to that person, and thereby, discusses philosophical ideas.

Seneca believes there are three kinds of life, namely, the life of theory, the life of politics (or practice), and the life of pleasure. He discusses how to choose one of these kinds of life, and summarizes the differences. He says that the life of theory is global, and the life of politics is local, but they both seek the best for mankind. The life of pleasure is self-seeking.

Seneca's reference to death is that what happened before I came to be will happen again after I die, so the time of suffering is now. We do not remember suffering before we were born, and so if we did not suffer then, we will not suffer after we die either. He said that before me and after me does not belong to me to worry about.

It is within man's power to become wise and virtuous, as man makes decisions for himself. He was one of the first philosophers to discuss man's will. He states that we must examine ourselves daily, and through this practice, we can move forward on the path to self-improvement. Emotions should never impede progress in becoming a wise and virtuous man. Virtue is truth that is immovable, and balance is the key to happiness. Attitude is more important than action, Seneca asserts. Being good is hard work.

While Seneca was one of the first Stoics, his philosophy was also uniquely his own, not matching the beliefs of other Stoics totally. He was somewhat of a hypocrite in that he said that he hated fame, yet he sought it; he argued poverty was best, yet he was wealthy.

CHAPTER 9: LAOZI

Do the difficult things while they are easy
and do the great things while they are small.
A journey of a thousand miles must begin
with a single step.

How important is meditation?

There are many stories about the Chinese philosopher Laozi, but his existence is not something that can be proven. Confucius and the Daoist tradition both share stories of Laozi. The name Laozi means "Old Master", and the tenets of Laozi have had a great impact on Chinese culture. The works attributed to Laozi were written as poems, and were translated into Sanskrit and Latin. It is believed that Laozi 's works are summaries of oral traditions.

The focus of Laozi's works is how to make this life significant. It describes a way of life characterized by simplicity, calmness, and freedom from the tyranny of desire. It discusses ethical and political advice intended for the ruling class to assure peace for the people. Laozi provides the foundation of Daoism, also called Taoism in Roman.

Daoism is concerned with following the Way or the Path in life, also called Dao. The philosophy focuses on understanding the nature of reality, increasing longevity, ordering life morally, practicing rulership, and regulating consciousness.

One should not interrupt the flow of reality and natural occurrences, according to Daoism. The way of heaven is always the way of good, not evil, and the way is simple. One works effortlessly in concert with God, or Dao. He does not discriminate against others, and is not distracted by society's constructs, but instead spontaneously follows the Path. It is possible to follow the path with meditative stillness, and this practice can leave to immorality, which is harmony and oneness with Dao.

PAXTON CASMIRO

CHAPTER 10: ST. THOMAS AQUINAS

How can we live in harmony? First we need to know we are all madly in love with the same God.

Who is God and who is Jesus Christ?

St. Thomas Aquinas was an Italian scholar in the Medieval period. He was born to parents of the nobility, and he was said to be a humble and peace-loving man. Against the wishes of his family, he gravitated toward the

Dominican order and eventually became a monk. He was named a saint fifty years after his death.

Aquinas believed that truth becomes known through both natural revelation, where people know truths through their human nature and through correct human reasoning, and supernatural revelation, which is faith-based knowledge revealed through scripture.

Aquinas asserted that God is simple, without composition of parts, such as body and soul, or matter and form. He also stated that God is perfect, lacking nothing. Also, God is infinite, and not limited in the ways that created beings are physically, intellectually, and emotionally; and God is immutable, incapable of change in His essence. Finally, he asserted that God is one, in His essence and his existence. He also believed that Jesus Christ was truly divine and not simply a human being or God merely inhabiting the body of Christ.

Aquinas also prevented proofs for what he believed. One of these proofs was the argument of the unmoved mover, which states that everything that is moved is moved by a mover; therefore, there must be a mover, and that mover is God. Another proof is the argument of the first cause, which states that everything that is caused is caused by something else; therefore, the cause of all things is God, who is uncaused, but has always been present.

The argument from contingency states that there are contingent beings in the universe which may either exist or not exist and, as it is impossible for everything in the universe to be contingent, that is coming from nothing, there must be a necessary being whose existence is not contingent on any other being, who is God. Another proof is the argument from degree, which states that there are various degrees of perfection which may be found throughout the universe, so there must be a pinnacle of perfection from which lesser degrees of perfection derive, which is God. The teleological argument or argument from design states that all natural bodies in the world act towards ends, which is characteristic of intelligence; therefore, there must be an intelligent being that guides all natural bodies towards their ends, which is God.

Aquinas defined the four cardinal virtues as prudence, temperance, justice and fortitude, which he held are natural and binding on everyone. In addition, there are three theological virtues, faith, hope and charity. He distinguished between four kinds of law: eternal law from God, natural law from human reason and interpretation of eternal law, human law, which is natural law applied by governments to societies, and divine law, the revealed law in the scriptures.

Aquinas' beliefs are still the foundation of the church, and his contributions toward ethics and law are invaluable. He created a system of classification for all types of knowledge.

CHAPTER 11: OCKHAM OR OCCAM

The explanation requiring the fewest assumptions is most likely to be correct.

How does one learn?

Ockham was an English philosopher who proposed a philosophy of simplicity, best expressed in his Ockham's Razor, which is quoted above. He states that entities are not to increase unless it is necessary, and that it is vanity to do with more what can be done with fewer. He believed that the simplest form of a statement is better than endless hypotheses.

Although ordained into the Franciscan order, he disagreed with St. Thomas of Aquinas in nearly all aspects, and was, therefore, condemned by the Catholic church. He believed that the priests should not give up their vow of poverty and own property, as the Pope declared was acceptable. He did believe that God exists, but it was only accepted through faith, and not able to be proven through reason. He believed that goodness is what God wills, rather than God willing something because it is good.

Politically, Ockham believed in the separation of church and state and the freedom of speech. However, he believed monarchy was the best form of governance, and did not support democracy. He argued for less secular power for the church.

Regarding learning, Ockham asserted that human beings are born blank slates who learn by observing qualities in objects. People learn by organizing their thoughts and connecting concepts. Unlike Aristotle, who thought there were ten states of being, Ockham believes that there are only two: substance and quality. He addressed language and the difference in direct reference and connotation in words. He brought rigor back into the study of logic. He asserted that logic is the analysis of scientific terms, but science is about things. Logic is concerned with universals and terms and concepts, and not physical states.

CHAPTER 12: MACHIAVELLI

It is better to be feared than loved, if you cannot be both.

Do the ends always justify the means?

Machiavelli is often equated with evil. He is credited with influencing Hitler and Stalin, and was a term used by Shakespeare to represent someone happy to sacrifice people for evil goals. Scholars debate whether Machiavelli's literary work *The Prince* was intended to be a guide to evil or a reflection of the world as he saw it. In any event, it is a philosophy of power and its methods and uses.

He felt that a good government was not

possible with the nature of mankind. He also believed that allowing religion to enter politics was destructive. He believed government, politics, and religion could not mesh in any way. He believed that a ruler must act in such a way or make decisions that a private citizen never would to accomplish goals for the good of the state. He advocated a dictatorship, and a dictator should use violence to maintain the existence of the state and political powers controlling that state. He said that a ruler must act as both a man and a beast, like a fox to discover traps and a lion to drive off wolves.

Machiavelli advised rulers wishing to take over another state to act quickly and with maximum force, leaving no one behind to challenge you in the future. He praised Cesare Borgia, who ruthlessly destroyed anyone he considered a threat to his power, and used him as an illustration of successful use of power.

Machiavelli stated that God would allow such action to create a strong and united state for the people's safety and prosperity.

Dependence on the noble class for support was foolish, he advised rulers, because then they would expect favors and just as quickly support someone to overthrow you. Likewise, the common people were not to be trusted because regardless of how long they lived under the control of the ruler, they would never forget the freedom that they once had and they would always be attempting to have that freedom again. Machiavelli believed that anyone with the ambition and ruthlessness to rule people had the right to do so. He maintained that these methods were ethical because the intention of having a strong, powerful state was worthy of any means necessary.

His later writings were more moderate

and he argued that a democratic republic would be the best type of government. He suggested that the best goals of a nation were independence, security, and a democratic constitution.

Machiavelli was born in Florence, and his father was a lawyer. He received an excellent education, studying Latin, rhetoric, and grammar. Hebecame an advisor in the government of Renaissance Florence.

CHAPTER 13:
FRANCIS BACON

A wise man will make more opportunities than he finds.

Does one need a hypothesis to make a discovery?

Francis Bacon believed that knowledge was power, and without power, effective action is impossible. He stated that only angels and God are spectators, and man must act. He believed that discovering ideas that would be useful was important. He argued that natural history, the scientific method, and practical knowledge were the things that were useful to aid man in living a better life.

He proposed that there were four idols, or erroneous thought processes of people. One of these is the idols of the tribe. This concept describes false notions that everyone has that are part of human nature. An example of this notion is the tendency of men to seek out evidence that supports what they already believe or the tendency to search for patterns. A second idol is the idols of the cave. These are conclusions that come about because of individual makeup and disposition. For example, some people are more positive and others are more negative and cautious. Third, the idols of the marketplace exist. This term explains the use of language and words and the array of meanings words can have. A fourth idol is the idols of the theater. This describes Bacon's belief that philosophies are no better than plays, superstition.

Bacon was a proponent of experimentation and observation. He believed scientific knowledge comes from repeated experiments. He advised checking conclusions with observations, but he did not talk about the value of a hypothesis. He was the first to propose use of inductive reasoning, using observation and data from observation to uncover laws and theories, as opposed to deductive reasoning, which uses logic. In his explanation of the process of inductive reasoning, he said that one must collect data and determine when the characteristic under investigation is present, when it is absent, and when it exists in varying degrees. Then, by examining the results, the researcher can decide which causes to reject and which causes are possible.

Bacon lived during the rise of science, with Galileo, Kepler, Issac Newton, and Thomas Hobbes. These inventors were called experimental philosophers.

Born into a wealthy family in London, England, Bacon was educated at home until he entered the Trinity College in Cambridge at the age of 11. After completing his studies, he began law school. He decided that the school was too old fashioned, so he left to become an assistant to the ambassador in France. Later he returned to London and completed law school. He was elected to Parliament and served 36 years. He was a political advisor, serving as Lord Chancellor until he pled guilty to accepting bribes and was arrested. He dedicated the remainder of his life to philosophy, living five more years.

CHAPTER 14: DESCARTES

If you would be a real seeker after truth, it is necessary that at least once in your life you doubt, as far as possible, all things.

Why does man contemplate God?

Descartes was a French philosopher, mathematician, and scientist. He is often called the "Father of Modern Philosophy". In addition to his important contributions to philosophy, he also is responsible for coordinate geometry, the Cartesian plane, astronomical advances, and optics. He studied at a Jesuit college and attended law school. He traveled around Europe, serving as a military engineer. He did not publish his first book because it contained the belief that the Earth revolved around the Sun, which was considered heresy by the church. He went to Holland to instruct Queen Christina in 1649, but died within a few months of arriving there.

Descartes stated that he had found a peaceful solitude, and in that place he was able to demolish all that he believed, all of his opinions, and start again forming his beliefs. While depending on science for his beliefs, he also recognized divine involvement in the world, meshing science and religion. He had three dreams or visions one night that radically changed everything that he believed, and these visions led to his peaceful solitude and reordering of life.

He believed firmly in the "method of doubt", that is, he believed that any information obtained from the senses was subject to doubt. He illustrated this fact with his assertion that a dream can be just as real and vivid as a real event. He believes that doubt is good, because it allows man to think and consider. Knowing is better than doubting, however. The difference in man and all other creatures is his ability to think and reason, and therefore, to ultimately know. His famous quotation, "I am thinking, therefore I am" reinforces this belief. While he could be a thinker without a body, he could never be a body without thought, he maintains. This framework of the separateness of mind and body is called dualism. He believed the mind and the body are two separate parts like two independent clocks keeping perfect time.

Descartes outlined four rules for thinking: never accept anything except clear, distinct ideas; divide all problems into as many parts as you can; order your thoughts from the simple to the complex; always check for oversights.

There are three main types of dualism: substance dualism, which differentiates between mental substances and material substances; property dualism, which describes mind and body as properties of material substances; and predicate dualism, which states that there is more than one way to determine a subject. Dualism is different from monism, which accepts mind and body as one whole.

All problems can be broken down into its simplest parts and be represented by abstract equations, according to Descartes. This method would allow objective reason to take over, rather than sensory perceptions, which are unreliable. Descartes described a great deceiver in this world who is always trying to trick people.

Thoughts of God are the Creator's mark on us, and he believed that God is benevolent, and He has given us our bodies and our minds, and He is perfect, He is not the deceiver to whom he refers. He attempted to rationally prove God exists, since reason is the only dependable way to know truth. He states that the reality of God's existence is a self-evident truth. Descartes believed that God implants moral principles in our minds, and these morals are innate.

CHAPTER 15: JOHN LOCKE

New opinions are always suspected, and usually opposed, without any other reason but because they are not already common.

Does creation prove God?

What rights does government have?

John Locke said that if one observes the world, he will see the marks of an extraordinary creator with wisdom and power. He will see the wonderful plan of creation, and if he reflects on his observations of nature, then he cannot miss the Deity, God. He says only an irrational man would deny God. Locke also said that reason must be the last judge and guide for our beliefs.

Locke was a philosopher, a political theorist, and a representative of the democratic revolution of his time in England. He was born in Somerset to a family of modest wealth. He studied medicine and chemistry at Oxford University. He became personal physician to the Earl of Shaftesbury, and saved his life by performing surgery on his liver. After reading Descartes, he became interested in philosophy, and his passion for philosophy took over his dedication to medicine.

Locke proposed that a newborn's mind is a blank slate. He senses the world around him, and develops ideas based on what he senses. He reflects on his thoughts, simple ones at first and then becoming more complex as the mind actively makes connections through comparing, contrasting, and making abstractions from those simple ideas. He states that objects have qualities, both primary and secondary qualities, that exist in the objects themselves. He contrasted the appearance of an object with its reality.

Morality is not innate, as many of the philosophers of the time believed, according to Locke. It only seems that these morals are innate because one does not remember when he first accepted them as truth. Children soak up whatever they are told, and only in adulthood, do some question their beliefs. People desire to have principles to live by, and that is the only desire that is innate, according to Locke.

Spiritual beliefs, according to Locke, are just composites of other ideas such as knowledge, power, and goodness. He states that we magnify these concepts into the idea of a Supreme Being. He states that belief in a Supreme Being is logical and natural, arising from the experiences of our lives. God cannot be proven, however.

Locke was fascinated with the concept of individual liberty. He says that the monarchy has no divine right to rule, since God did not place some men above others. He asserts that all men are equal. He states that all men can use reason to know moral law, and no one should harm another in his life, health, liberty, or profession. He believed that the right to own property was implied by natural law because of labor. One's labor is his own, and anything he makes with his labor should be his as well. He says that man has the right to kill in protection of his property. Locke states that government was created because of property, and because of the inalienable rights ordained by God; specifically, the right to life, liberty, and property. In addition, one has the right to protest against unjust rulers and laws.

Locke's political philosophy also included the idea of checks and balances between the king and the legislature. He stated that there should be a separation of power, and the legislature should be supreme. The legislature should be able to be removed by the people, and the executive, be it king or president, could be forcibly removed if he refuses to listen to the people. He said that force should only be used against unjust and unlawful force.

Locke was very concerned with using precise language and clarity in communication.

CHAPTER 16: LEIBNIZ

The worst enemy you can meet is yourself; you lie in wait for yourself in canyons and forests.

Do things always work out for the best?

Gottfried Leibniz was a German philosopher and mathematician whose philosophical views are said to exemplify rationalism. He invented differential calculus, and he wrote on many other subjects as well. He wrote essays on the goodness of God, the freedom of man, and the origin of evil which make up his book *Theodicy*. His proofs of the role of the Supreme Being, God, were designed to refute those who pictured the world run by an indifferent and impersonal force and natural laws.

Leibniz asserts that we live in the best of all possible worlds because of the perfection of God. The world is organized according to reason and fulfillment of one's desires is not the way to happiness. Our world is one of pre-established harmony, and it is full of meaning.

While man is not like God, with perfection, God allows grace to lift people up when they are imperfect. Man has freedom of will, and the choices one has made in the past creates the present reality for a person. However, He believed that everything in life does work out for the best in all circumstances.

Leibniz contributed to the understanding of reason with three fundamental principles. One of these principles is the identity/contradiction theory. If a proposition is true, its opposite must be false and vice-versa. Another principle is sufficient reason, which states that in order for any event to occur or truth to evolve, there has to be a reason, even if this reason is known only to God. The third principle is referred to as Leibniz's Law. It states that if two things are distinct from one another, they cannot have every property in common. For example, if X has every characteristic Y has, then Y is X and not separate, but identical.

Leibniz believes in the law of

continuity, as well. This law states that nature never takes great leaps, but is always sequential. No movement can come from total rest, but nature goes forward step-by-step. Instead of believing that everything was made of one substance like his contemporaries, Leibniz proposed that there were an infinite number of substances, which he referred to as "monads." He said that each monad is different, but each mirrors the universe but is not located in space or time. Nothing goes into or out of a monad, he continued to explain. Each monad is immaterial and has a soul, but monads cannot interact with each other. They appear to act together only because of a pre-established harmony ordained by God.

Leibniz was the eternal optimist, believing God always chooses the best for man.

CHAPTER 17:
HUME

Beauty in things exists only in the mind which contemplates them.

Does philosophy have any real value?

David Hume was born in Edinburgh

of Scottish parents, he became an important literary figure, and wrote a history of England. He was a philosopher who published his most important philosophical work at the age of 28. He wrote of understanding, passions, and morals. He believed man's ability to reason is a result of language abilities, and that human nature results from the brain and nervous system. He believed one thing does not cause another, but it is simply the mind drawing connections between events. Knowledge, Hume says, is in fact tradition and custom. These things simply allow life to be easier for man.

While many of Hume's philosophical ideas are negative, refuting both philosophy and religion as insufficient for providing answers to life, he did contribute understanding of thinking. Hume identifies three tools used for philosophical inquiry, the microscope, the razor, and the fork. The microscope is the ability to break down an idea into its simplest form. This is required to understand a concept. The razor states that if the idea cannot be broken down, then it has no value, and the razor signifies the need to cut it out of thought. The fork stands for the idea that truths can be separated into two types. One of these is the truth that once things are proven true, they remain true. The other truth relates to events that occur in the world.

Hume, in his treatise on passion, states that original impressions, or emotions, are internal and come from physical sources. However, passions are secondary impressions that exist as direct passions like grief, fear, and joy, and as indirect passions like love and hate. It is pleasure and pain that motivate people and create passions, which in turn initiates action.

Regarding morals, Hume states that morals cannot be based on reason. They come only from the affection man feels for one another. He states that beliefs are based on the connection among objects, and only if of interest to the person. He differentiates between virtue and vice, defining virtue as pleasure and vice as pain. Something is moral or immoral based on how it affects others; therefore, it can only be seen from a social point of view. The foundation of moral obligation, Hume says, is sympathy. Those without sympathy or empathy commit the worst crimes, he states.

CHAPTER 18: ROUSSEAU

Patience is bitter, but its fruit is sweet.

Is society a chain or an anchor on man?

Rousseau was born of humble parents in Calvinist Geneva, and his mother died shortly after his birth. Abandoned by his father by the age of twelve, he went from relative to relative. Finally, he ran away at the age of 16, and some say it was because he had converted to Catholicism. He traveled around Europe, and he was often seen in the company of noble women of the time. He became secretary to the French ambassador until he met a servant girl in Paris, and he lived with her until his death. They had five children, and he took all five to the orphanage to be raised by others.

Rousseau believed that both art and science had degraded man. He believed that science and virtue were not possible to exist together. He asserted that man was basically good, but that he was changed into bad by institutions of society. He discussed a "noble savage", one who was primitive, but unspoiled by society. He believed primitive man was in harmony with nature, but civilized man was cut off from nature and from himself. He advocated for education for children where the mind was developed without destruction of his natural state.

Rousseau is best known for his social contract theory, which states that when men come into the world, they are free; however, society acts as a chain on man's freedom. He believed that the only legitimate form of government is one in which all people agree on its form and its purpose is self-preservation. He provided the foundational truth on which democracy is based, namely, government by "the consent of the governed." He believed transparency of government was a necessary quality of a righteous government.

He stated that we have free will, and that is good, but we do not always know how to act. He says we have to be careful not to become subject to another's will, or we lose our freedom. He advised putting the heart before reason, poetry before science, and focusing on emotion and imagination were the best ways to act. His writings formed the foundation of the literary period of romanticism. He wrote ballets, operas, and a play, as well as his other literary texts.

Self-preservation and pity, according to Rousseau are man's only two motivations to act. Giving up one's personal freedom for the good of the people is the only legitimate loss of freedom.

CHAPTER 19: HEGEL

To help bring philosophy closer to the form of Science, to the goal where it can lay aside the title 'love of knowing' and be 'actual knowing'- that is what I have set myself to do.

How can technology help mankind fulfill his purpose?

Hegel believed that the modern world has what mankind has long wanted, and rather than believing technology, freedom, and capitalism harm mankind, they can fulfill his need to express his consciousness. Hegel did not believe that there was only one philosophy that is correct, but a combination of views depict truth. He saw science as an explanation of our consciousness over time and history is the process of discovering great truths within ourselves. Truth is not just what one can see physically, but includes the unseen reasoning behind what is observed as well, according to Hegel. The only real data includes an understanding of that data.

Hegel asserts that the observer and the observed are one, and our consciousness is part of science as well. He differentiates between absolute and relative reality, stating that relative knowledge is things and their connection to each other while absolute knowledge exists in isolation. The way that we need to approach science is to break everything down into smaller and smaller pieces, and then to put it back together with understanding. One person is not important in the great scheme of the universe, however. He says that personal happiness comes when one realizes his individuality is not a real thing, and having a body is only temporary; therefore, suffering is temporary as well.

Hegel states that the world focuses on reason, but man's unwillingness to study philosophy makes religion a necessity. The foundation of life in philosophical terms becomes God in the religious view. Philosophy and religion are not rivals, but they are both aspects of the same truth.

Hegel worked as a tutor in Berne and Frankfurt, and then became a university lecturer and editor. He wrote treatises on his philosophical views and became a professor at the University of Berlin.

CHAPTER 20:
KANT

Science is organized knowledge. Wisdom is organized life.

If everyone has different experiences, how can learn truth through experience?

Immanuel Kant was a Prussian scholar and philosopher who became a professor at the university in Konigsberg. He was a man of routine, and people were said to set their watches by his daily walks. He was influenced by Leibniz and Hume.

Kant was said to be the greatest of

modern philosophers, and he explained his view of how the human mind works. He believed one should look inward rather than outward to understand the world. Kant differentiated between phenomena, or appearance, which is the way our mind interprets what we see, and noumena, or reality, things that exist whatever our minds think. He is described as an ideal transcendentalist in his views, one who believes that the world is composed not of physical things, but of ideas, and one can never transcend the limitations of the mind to know the world.

Kant believed that our mind assimilates knowledge into categories, like causation. Because our brains work to find causes, we cannot help but see causes in the world. He used the terms "analytic" and "synthetic" to differentiate between propositions. He described analytic terms as descriptive terms, but synthetic terms go beyond description to show cause and effect. He also used the term "a priori" to describe knowledge coming from reason and "a posteriori" as knowledge coming from experience.

The morality of something is determined by the motive behind the action. If something cannot be shown to be good by using reason, then it probably is not good. He believed that it was right for us to try to discover natural laws and moral law. He discussed the existence of an iron law which he called the "categorical imperative." He said that this categorical imperative could never be broken, regardless of the circumstance. Kant believed that moral law is as real as the physical world, and this law comes from God. He said the categorical imperative is true globally. He believed that God is the source of an absolute and unconditional moral truth, and this truth filled him with awe. The existence of God cannot be proven or disproven.

Kant said we should treat people as ends in themselves, never as means to an end. This truth is similar to the Golden rule, and it can be known by reason.

Achieving happiness is a legitimate goal for mankind, according to Kant, but living against moral law would lead to unhappiness. Doing one's duty was more important than the quest for happiness, however. He believed that one must do what makes him worthy of happiness, and he will be happy.

Kant insisted that reason can supply

absolute ethical principles, absolute universal truths. He believed that reason can discover eternal principles just as reason can lead to truths in math and geometry. Just as the same mathematics is true in every country, so are moral truths, according to Kant. It does not matter if the ethical principles are found by observation or experiment or preferences, they are still truths because of reason. Ethical truths are universal and absolute, with no room for compromise.

Man is able to follow these rational dictates because he is able to use willpower, a special gift from God. Our capacity of free will elevates man above all other creatures. We, like no other creature, can overcome desire and follow the demands of moral law, according to Kant.

CHAPTER 21: JOHN STUART MILL

A person may cause evil to others not only by his actions but by his inaction, and in either case he is justly accountable to them for the injury.

Liberty is important for mankind because with personal liberty, all questions are open to debate and reasoning and advancement, so all society benefits, according to Mill. While many governments were democratic during the life of Mill, he stated that democracy was no guarantee of personal freedom. He spoke of the "tyranny of the majority" limiting personal freedom with its demand for conformity.

Mill believed that people should enjoy

all personal freedom, as long as it does not hurt another person. He spoke specifically about the freedom of conscience, thoughts and feelings, tastes and pursuits, associations with others, and the right to publish our opinions. He believed that it is human nature to want to impose our will on others, and therefore, government will attempt to take away more personal freedoms and personal liberty will erode without constant monitoring of government.

Individuality is the key to a successful government, Mill asserted, because it is in the myriad views of the individuals that great ideas appear.

Mill stated that pleasure is both quantitatively different for different people and qualitatively different for different people. He stated that he had rather be a dissatisfied person than a satisfied pig.

Mill was born in London, and received an extensive education. He was not allowed to play with other children, so had learned Greek by three years of age and Latin by age eight. By twelve he had mastered logic, and by sixteen, he taught economics. He wrote on the system of logic as well as other topics. He was an avid social reformer and author and editor of many books and articles.

CHAPTER 22: KIERKEGAARD

Life is not a problem to be solved, but a reality to be experienced.

What are you willing to risk to follow your passion?

Kierkegaard was a proponent of individualism, and he said that every man can be great in his own way, according to what he loves and what he expects. He describes a knight of faith as one who risks his entire life on what he values, on love or on a task. In contrast is one who just completes one task after another with no passion. He says that one can lose himself quietly without notice. He says if one loses an arm or leg or $5, he is distraught, but he can lose himself and barely notice.

Kierkegaard is referred to as an existentialist, one who believes that philosophy should focus on the human experience. Free will, personal responsibility, and choice which enables one to seek what he loves is the essence of human experience.

The highest form of life, he believed, was to replace doubt with faith. He wrote about the Old Testament's Abraham in *Fear and Trembling*, and speaks with awe of Abraham's willingness to sacrifice his only son Issac in total faith in God. Because he was willing to do the absurd just because God required it, he is representative of the best of men.

Kierkegaard states that life can only be understood by looking back, but that it must be lived going forward. One must be an ethical man and an aesthetic man, but he also must make a leap of faith.

Kierkegaard was born into a religious family in Copenhagen, Denmark, and he was expected to study theology at the university, but turned to philosophy instead. He was engaged to be married, but stated publicly that philosophy was more important than his fiancé and marriage, so he was breaking the engagement.

CHAPTER 23: KARL MARX

Religion is the sigh of the oppressed creature, the heart of a heartless world, just as it is the spirit of a spiritless situation. It is the opium of the people.

Does society work better when the resources of production are privately owned or collectively owned?

Karl Marx was a Prussian who attended the University of Berlin, and there joined a radical group who opposed the religious and political establishments of the time. For his doctorate, Marx wrote his dissertation on ancient Greek philosophy, but he was denied a teaching position because of his radical ideas. He became a journalist, where he worked for one radical newspaper after another. As his writing became even more radical, he was expelled from Belgium, France, and refused readmission to Prussia. He settled in London and there helped establish the Communist League. His most famous work was *Das Kapital*, a work on economics.

In this work, Marx states that a key part of one's sense of happiness and self-concept is labor. Turning raw materials into something of value is an expression of creativity and a display of identity. Marx expounds on these ideas, stating that a worker under capitalism which is based on private ownership of resources takes away self-worth of the laborer. In capitalism, the laborer loses his pleasure in work and sees it only as a way to survive. The capitalist does not desire commodities, but only money, he says.

Marx differentiates between the use value of a commodity and the exchange value of a product. The use value is the value of the product to fulfill needs, and the exchange value is its value when sold measured in money. He states that a commodity's value should not depend on supply and demand, but on the laborer's work in creating the product. He then goes on to develop the concept of exploitation of the worker.

Marx describes a new mode of production that will arise out of realization of the workers of this exploitation, and this new mode will involve collective ownership of resources and be called Communism.

Marx is responsible for the return of materialism for the philosophers of his time. His philosophy and thought process change over time, but his transition from humanist to historical materialist is clear.

CHAPTER 24:
WILLIAM JAMES

Act as if what you do makes a difference.
It does.

What is your personal philosophy?

William James was an American who studied to be a physician and psychologist. He clarified and publicized pragmatism, the belief that philosophy should not look at the "first" things, like principles and categories, but the "last" things, like consequences and facts.

Every person has a philosophy,

according to James, which is a sense of what life means to that individual, which is developed from books and experience, and results in a personal bias. He says that each person's philosophy falls into two categories: the empiricist, who believes in facts and observations and the rationalist, who believes in the abstract and eternal. He states that pragmatism is different from either of these categories, combining the best of both categories. He states that the pragmatist can be open to truths about God, and the ultimate truth can be examined to see what difference it will make in the world. James focuses on the myriad diversity of the world and the power of individuality.

James took philosophy and split off into a new science, psychology. In his two works in psychology, he examines thinking and how people think. He explains that thoughts belong to the individual, that thoughts are always changing, that thoughts are sequential in some fashion, and that thoughts deal with objects that the mind chooses as its focus. He called his description of the mind stream of consciousness.

There is more than one self, according to James. There is the me; the material me, which includes my body and belongs; the social me, which refers to interpersonal relationships; and the spiritual me, which refers to one's personality, character, and values.

There is also a pattern to one's thinking, according to James. The pattern begins with sensation, which becomes a perception. The perception leads to imagination, where we think of past experiences related to this one and future experiences with this phenomenon. Imagination leads to belief, which is the sense that sensations are reality.

James traces the origin of emotion. He says that we have a perception, which is followed by a physical response. This physical response leads to an emotion. An example is one hearing a noise in the dark. This perception of danger immediately causes one's heart to be faster, breathing to slow, and senses to become sharper. These physical changes lead to the emotion of fear.

James also categorizes decision-making into five kinds. He describes the reasonable sort, where we accept rational arguments, and the sort that is triggered by external circumstances, such as overhearing a rumor. A third sort is caused by our submission to something within ourselves, such as a habit, and the fourth, the sort that results from a sudden change of mood. The last is the rarest sort of decision making, the sort that is a consequence of our own voluntary choice.

James says that there are two viewpoints to life and belief. One is positive, and one is negative. Those who are negative fear making a mistake, and are miserly with accepting new ideas, and those who are positive embrace all truths and are generous with truth. He states that one has to meet reality halfway with a leap of faith, which he calls precursive faith, that which runs ahead of the evidence.

CHAPTER 25: NIETZSCHE

That which does not kill us makes us stronger.

When you look into an abyss, the abyss also looks into you.

What happens if one believes in nothing?

Nietzsche is known as a nihilist. He declared that God is dead, and believed that one should abandon all beliefs. He believed that science would replace both Christianity and atheism. He believed that there is no absolute truth, but truth comes from flexibility and acceptance of many ideas. He felt that the search for real truth was a waste of time. He accused Christianity of smothering everything with its life-denying pieties, but never providing a real moral basis for mankind. He said it is the morality of the herd, a slave mentality. True virtue is for the aristocratic few, and the concept of morality for all people is absurd.

Nietzsche described a superman, one who desires power and a higher state of bring. This superman reevaluates all morals, and becomes a man of strength, hardness, and even cruelty. He states that man should be trained for war and women for the recreation of man, and all else is foolish. He says that the future is in the hands of this great man.

Nietzsche focused on the constant change of life. He said that truth is constantly changing, ethics are constantly changing, values are constantly changing, and man himself is constantly changing. He believed that the world is cyclical and ever changing. Man must embrace change because that is part of being. Truth is relative, and there is no absolute truth, he says.

Despising democracy, Christianity, and greatness of man, Nietzsche believed that just being and seeking a life free of pain and fear is all one could hope for.

Nietzsche was a Prussian whose father and grandfather were Lutheran ministers. He attended boarding school and university, where he was recognized as a brilliant scholar. He was appointed professor of classics at the University of Basel at the age of 24. His health was poor, and he had a nervous breakdown, after which he lived for eleven years in a vegetative state.

CHAPTER 26: HEIDEGGER

Why are there beings at all instead of nothing? That is the question.

Do you make your own decisions or do you follow the expectations of society?

Heidegger states that the question of 'being' has been discussed by many philosophers through the ages, but that it had never been answered with satisfaction. He says that the concept of being is "shrouded in darkness." He says that being can be expressed as 'Dasein', self-reflective consciousness. He says that the debate among philosophers about what we can really know is irrelevant, because being in the world is all that matters. Man has the ability to search, make, and build, and that is what matters as the man develops.

Heidegger divides observation of the world into three parts: looking around, considering others, and looking through others and into ourselves. The observation of the world should result in questioning oneself and exploring where one is in the world. Life is about our possibilities in the environment we are in, he says. He calls this 'thrownness', that is that we are cast into a particular place, time, and family, and we had no part in deciding these issues; therefore, our role is making sense of this fall into a place. We can do this by our speech and actions, and we have a responsibility to do something with our lives.

Our moods and emotions are not just brief states that we enter, but are central to our being. Moods allow us to respond to the world, and with moods, we cannot remain neutral. Our moods make us attuned to the world around us, and we constantly make adjustments based on our moods, whether we are in tune with the world or out of tune being the motivation for our actions.

Heidegger discusses authenticity as recognizing that one is free to make his or her own decisions and is not bound by society's expectations. Of course, everyone is limited by society's rules and, therefore, their authenticity exists only to a certain degree. The most important part of my existence is that my life is mine.

The source of the anxiety that men feel is the realization that this is not our home. We feel isolation, but we continue with life in spite of that, realizing that we play a unique role in this world. Man's view is future oriented, according to Heidegger, and therefore, he is always looking ahead to our possibilities.

Heidegger was born in Germany into a conservative Catholic family. He entered a seminary at 14 to enter the priesthood, but he left to pursue his studies in literature and philosophy. He became a professor after receiving his PhD in philosophy.

CHAPTER 27: SARTRE

Everything has been figured out, except how to live.

Why is romantic love so popular to man?

Sartre divided the world into things that have consciousness and things that do not. He believed that humans, who have consciousness, have no essential essence. He states that when one examines and analyzes one's self, what he finds is nothing, but there is good in that. One is free to create the self or the life that he wants, totally from that nothingness.

Sartre believed that man is responsible for himself and for his world. He states that we are abandoned in the universe, but we can see everything as an opportunity to define who we are. He believes that success is worthless, but freedom is everything, even if it is a burden that many seek to escape from through self-deception. Consistency is also worthless, because one needs to constantly experience new things and leave security behind.

Sartre believed that man is free to make decisions, and he should take existential leaps in to the unknown. He stated that relationships are so important to us because we need others to see us and make us real, states Sartre. The best chance for happiness in a relationship is to give the other total freedom, even though it is in man's nature to want to "own" the other person, not the person himself, but his will to want us. He believed that romantic love is so powerful because the other person fills a hole within us.

Sartre was born in Paris, France. His father died when he was a baby and he was raised by his mother, who was a cousin of philosopher and missionary Albert Schweitzer, and his grandfather, who was a doctor. He was well educated, being awarded the Nobel Prize for literature in 1964, but refusing it. He became more political as he got older.

CHAPTER 28: HANNAH ARENDT

Forgiveness is the key to action and freedom.

What is mankind's glory?

Hannah Arendt was born in Germany, and studied theology. With the Nazi party's rise in Germany, she fled to Paris and there was involved in Zionist organizations and rescued Jewish children in Austria and Czechoslovakia. She and her husband were placed in German concentration camps in France, but escaped to the United States, where she became an American citizen.

Arendt was an expert in Greek and Roman philosophy, and her works express her background in philosophy. She asserted that nature is cyclical with birth, living, and death being inevitable, but humans are free to act, and this is man's glory. She writes of Jesus of Nazareth's emphasis on action and forgiveness, and this forgiveness gives us the power for redemption.

One's creativity confirms his uniqueness and the power to impact his world, according to Arendt. She describes three basic activities: the labor of life itself, work which is permanence and durability, and action, which requires no things or matter, so is the essence of being human. Arendt says that labor is the activity of living, growing, and ultimately, decaying. It is the essence of life itself. Work, however, is an unnatural activity performed in nature, which can outlast this world. It leaves some permanence, defying time. Action also transcends the natural world.

The home, rather than the public arena, is the focal point of life in our time, and this private domain has its own benefits. Arendt proclaims that love has the greatest power, and it is our glory revealed. People live together, not just for emotional and material support, but for the pleasure of seeing others reflect one's own identity. Who we are is revealed in our words and deeds, and by spending time with someone, we can reveal who we really are.

Our ability to act gives our lives constant new beginnings, Arendt asserts, constantly providing new hope and faith. The faith comes from the realization that people can act and change. However, we must beware that we do not abandon our individuality and just become a reflection of the society around us and our environment. Instead of tackling the problem of living head on, she says, and living and acting for ourselves, we have to be careful not to just become a consumer with preferences.

CHAPTER 29: A. J. AYER

Philosophy, as it is written, is full of questions... which seem to be factual but are not.

Are morals based on reasoning or emotion?

Ayer was born in 1910, and attended Eton College and Oxford. He studied philosophy and was a professor, as well as a major media figure. When Ayer was only 22 years old, he met with the Vienna Circle, which was a group of physicists, mathematicians, and philosophers, who had a massive effect on modern thought.

One of the conclusions that Ayers made is the principle of verification, which states that a sentence has meaning if it has a truth that corresponds to an observable situation. If a statement is likely true, and can be confirmed as such, it is meaningful. Universal laws are true because of induction and repeated observations. Statements about morality are based on values that are driven by emotion and are, therefore, meaningless. Most language says more about the speaker than it does about reality, according to Ayer.

CHAPTER 30: MICHAEL MCMAHON

The family circle has widened. The whirlpool of information fathered by electric media... far surpasses any possible influence mom and dad can now bring to bear. Character is no longer shaped by only two earnest, fumbling experts. Now all the world's a sage.

How has today's media changed man?

Michael McLuhan was born in Canada, the son of a Baptist schoolteacher and real estate salesman. He earned his degree in English, and became a teaching assistant at the University of Wisconsin. His reputation grew as he published books on modern life.

McLuhan was the originator of the phrases "global village" and "the medium is the message." There was a typographical error and the title of his book became *The Medium is the Massage.* He liked the title because he said it fit as "all media does give us a workover."

McLuhan's philosophy states that children are taught words and meanings and these make a child act and think in certain ways. Likewise, the advent of printing made man more fragmented and detached. Technology and the electronic age have created communication and the internet that have brought man together again with friends and connections with others. Man has gone from a few hundred books in his library to millions of books via the internet. Letters and words made man primarily use the eye to take in the world, but now multimedia uses all our senses to bring knowledge to us. We are bombarded with information, and we cannot organize it in our brains quickly enough, so we pay attention to patterns.

The means that we take in information is deeply changing man and changing what is known. Man is reconsidering and reevaluating every thought, action, and institution we formerly knew. Even children are exposed to so much information and adult concepts that childhood is no longer the same.

That which is public and that which is private have changed tremendously with the advent of social media, and while some leaders think that is a positive, McLuhan questioned its meaning. If one is not constantly updating information about self on line, who is self and is there a self, he questions. If there is new technology, it changes the way man thinks and changes his mindset.

Regarding work, McLuhan says that the conventional idea of jobs are an outgrowth of the industrial revolution and specialization, but are no longer the same. Now experts who participate in freelancing, consultant work will become the norm, made possible by the internet.

Politics has also changed because of modern media, with an audience now replacing the 'public.' Knowing what is going on around the world constantly and reacting to those events with emotions requires a sense of commitment and participation with others. Teamwork replaces individual effort in the new technological world.

CHAPTER 31: DAVID BOHM

Thus, the classical idea of the separability if the world into distinct but interacting parts is no longer valid or relevant. Rather, we have to regard the universe as an undivided and unbroken whole.

Is the universe a "thing" or is it energy?

Bohm attended the University of Pennsylvania and then the University of California, where he worked in theoretical physics. He was recommended to work on the atomic bomb at Los Alamos, but his involvement with radical politics prevented his participation. Instead, he taught at Berkeley and Princeton, where he worked alongside Albert Einstein. After being called before McCarthy's Un-American Activities Committee, he was fired from Princeton and arrested. Even after he was acquitted, he was unable to regain his position. He moved to Israel, and there discovered an important effect of the ability of particles to sense magnetic fields.

As a physicist, Bohm was not only concerned about his discoveries, but he was also concerned with the effect of his ideas on mankind. He believed that many of the world's problems came from the belief that every person is separate from others, and that we, therefore, need to defend ourselves from others.

Bohm's view of the universe was that we should view matter as a form of energy rather than a collection of tiny particles. He states that everything is a unified field and always in motion. Every field merges with other fields. This is Bohm's view of wholeness.

Within his view of wholeness, Bohm sees all can be divided into implicate and explicate orders. The explicate order is everything that we can perceive with our senses, everything that is real that exists in time and space. The implicate order is outside of space and time and is the essence of the explicate. The implicate and the explicate are part of the unbroken and undivided totality of the universe.

Bohm notes that long ago, man

separated the physical from thoughts, not because it was truth, but due to convenience. If they both are part of the whole, how can they be separate? Likewise, the scientist, the observed, the tools used for observing, and the results of experiments are all part of the same thing. Therefore, if we reflect on our own thoughts or meditate, we will know what reality is, and we will realize that we are all part of one whole, and it will change the way we relate to others. Thoughts are based on memory and can be wrong, but flashes of insight can come that let us see our thoughts are wrong, and he called this "intelligent perception." We can know something without knowing how we know it, and this is our mind getting in tune with the universe. He states that we are not independent and separate but like ripples in a current.

CHAPTER 32: IRIS MURDOCH

We need a moral philosophy in which the concept of love, so rarely mentioned now by philosophers, can once again be made central.

What should our focus be in life?

Iris Murdoch spoke against existentialism, which was the philosophy of the time, as well as behaviorism and utilitarianism. Instead, she said that developing one's inner self was the goal of man. She believed that Good, a reality without form that underlies the universe, is what men seek subconsciously. She believed that Good is the central concept to man's morals and the universe itself. She says that modern man is aware of who he is and what he wants out of life, focused on results and public acclaim, yet his mental life is without meaning because an individual's will is all that matters to modern man. She says man's focus should be looking at his fellow man in the most loving way and the highest light, and this requires obedience.

Murdoch states that morality is concrete and universal, and it is in a totally different realm than science. Science is not separate from culture, but science is part of culture; however, science and culture come after morality. Literature is the lens through which we understand all of these concepts. One is to be true to what one sees and loves, and art is important, which goes against philosophies of the time which call art a luxury that indulges man's lack of reason.

Murdoch believes that we must reduce the size of our ego, and we can do this by appreciating beauty and truth, in nature, art, and literature. She defines freedom as a disciplined overcoming of oneself. Man's quest of finding oneself is a misguided approach to life, because if one's self is found, she says it will be small and of little interest.

Murdoch was born in 1919, and she grew up loving animals, singing, and reading. She read philosophers from history, and wrote about philosophy and philosophers, as well as other important modern works.

CHAPTER 33:
THOMAS KUHN

All historically significant theories agree with the facts, but only more or less.

What is a paradigm and how does it come about?

Thomas Kuhn was finishing his PhD at Harvard when he began to teach the history of science for nonscientists. He changed his views of science in preparing to teach and teaching the course, and this knowledge changed his career path. He became focused on the history of science, and he wrote several books on scientists and scientific discoveries. One conclusion that he made in the book was that paradigms, where worldviews are adjusted, come in science and other disciplines as well, and are, in fact, very important in understanding the world.

Kuhn states that textbooks give facts and theories, but scientific discoveries and experimental results do not occur in such a step-by-step way. He notes that specific people do not go about making wonderful discoveries, but that the scientific community and intellectual changes of a time are just as critical to the discoveries as the man or woman credited with a discovery.

He describes a paradigm as a universally recognized scientific achievement for a particular time period. When a new discovery is made, it does not just add on to what is new, but changes the entire framework of science. When a new paradigm replaces an older one, the entire world seems to change. He says that a paradigm can be honest, but it can also be wrong. The human desire for certainty and consistency makes it hard for man to accept new paradigms.

When a paradigm no longer explains new findings of scientists, then the paradigm is in crisis, and a new paradigm can be created. However, scientists accept that the scientific community is correct, and they are willing to defend the current beliefs. If some truth or finding does not fit current accepted thought, then scientists will ignore that finding and call it a mistake. He calls these findings "violations of expectation", and they rarely change the established paradigm.

Scientists, according to Kuhn, are not creative thinkers, and they often spend their careers working on smaller topics within the established paradigm to make that paradigm even more accepted. He says that if a finding is outside the box, it will not even be seen by scientists. However, infrequently, scientific revolutions occur as new paradigms and major changes in how we see facts occur. They never happen because of the work of one man or overnight. Paradigm shifts occur as a process that is a slow acceptance of a new framework of knowledge. Science, therefore, is not on a path of progress for mankind, but differences in thinking.

CHAPTER 34: MICHAEL FOUCAULT

The sciences are well made languages.

Are science and other disciplines a linear addition of facts and knowledge?

Foucault was born in France, and his father was a physician. His father expected him to become a physician as well, but he was more interested in literature and history. He eventually received degrees in philosophy, psychology, and psychiatry, and he was a professor in France and Sweden, as well as an author of books on philosophy, political movements, and the history of sexuality.

Foucault states that knowledge is a cultural product with different disciplines expressing the overall world view of the time. He says that our minds prefer a linear arrangement of knowledge, seeing most disciplines as a series of additional knowledge added to the same body of knowledge as previously. However, he says this does not describe reality. Reality is that a certain time period develops the knowledge in the disciplines as a reflection of the current culture. He says that we possess ways of seeing and thinking that make it impossible to think in new, different ways. We do not see things objectively, but base our views and truth on our current categorization system.

Science and other disciplines do not have a starting point and new discoveries building on that belief, but that the culture and intellectual beliefs of the era coalesce into the body of knowledge that is accepted in that era. It is not what writers of an era say that is important, but how they say it that is important, he asserts. A "ground of knowledge" can suddenly disappear, and a new ground can appear in a different place.

CHAPTER 35: JEAN BAUDRILLARD

We live in a world where there is more and more information, and less and less meaning.

Why do we shop?

Jean Baudrillard was the first in his family to attend university, and he wrote nine books that modern philosophy is still processing and absorbing. He considered himself a sociologist, rather than a philosopher.

Baudrillard 's philosophy is an antithesis to traditional Western philosophy.

He focuses on self, free will, and knowledge, and discusses living the authentic life. He believed man is not an individual, but simply a unit reflecting whatever is happening in media. He saw man as consumer, not individual. He believed if something could not be reproduced and shared, it was meaningless. He believes that reality conforms to our beliefs. He disavowed duality such as being and appearance and reality and concept, but states that what is real is what can be reproduced on a computer endlessly, even if it has no basis in rationality or truth. He says we have substituted the signs, the imitation, the duplication, the parody for the real.

Baudrillard describes the new world as hyperreal, and it eliminates the need for the imaginary. We are left with a giant simulation in place of real life. With the prevalence of the abstract and hyperreal, a value of reality is inflated. We cherish museums and their preservation of the past as a reflection of our hope that there is a reality.

Baudrillard attacks capitalism, as most modern philosophers do, but he does not just describe it as immoral, but as a "monstrous enterprise." The focus on economic indicators and demand make these the core of our society, and in doing so, makes any distinction between true and false and good and evil disappear. We are no longer free willed citizens, but we are just consumers.

Political activities, such as elections and presidential actions, are simply a drama on stage for spectators, citizens, he says. The more media focuses on these political actions and figures, the more evidence there is that this is just a charade, and the more people hate politics, the more intense the media coverage of it will grow. He says that television is what renders what is true and what is not. The movie of an event becomes more real to people than the actual event.

Baudrillard says that a hyperreal culture needs frequent sacrifices, and the more popular one is, the more likely he is to become a sacrifice. He questions whether media is on the side of power and manipulating the masses, or is it on the side of liquidating meaning. Does the constant violence on television make violence no longer real? he asks.

Commodities, material goods, are no longer of value, he says, but what is important are the stories and images associated with the goods. We do not shop to get items, but we shop to fit in our culture.

Philosophers have long argued about the difference between subject and object, viewer and object viewed, but Baudrillard sees that argument as no longer significant. The object is what is important now, and not just the object, but a media representation of the object; the subject is irrelevant. Man is simply a machine that consumes and reproduces media representations.

CHAPTER 36: HARRY FRANKFURT

One of the most salient features of our culture is that there is so much bullshit. Everyone knows this. Each of us contributes his share. But we tend to take the situation for granted. Most people are rather confident of their ability to recognize bullshit and to avoid being taken in by it. So the phenomena has not aroused much deliberate concern, not attracted much sustained inquiry. In consequence, we have no clear understanding

of what bullshit is, why there is so much of it,
and what function it serves.

What is bullshit?

Harry Frankfurt was a philosophy professor at Princeton, who discussed the frequency with which modern man encounters "bullshit," which he describes as an attempt to mislead, but it is not quite a lie. He states that a lie has a specific intent, but "bullshit" is spinning a story. It is unconcerned with facts or truth, but is more dangerous than lies because a lie starts with a truth, but "bullshit" does not. He says that it is more prevalent now because people attempt to talk about what they know nothing about. We cannot fit in our society if we say that we do not know something; instead, we have to make up stories. It is no longer important to be correct, just sincere.

Not only does an individual "bullshit", but organizations and governments do as well. Frankfurt says that this is a corruption of humanity. Rejection of the authority of truth and replacing it with a story or a "fast sell" can lead to the rise of Hitlers and Madoffs, whose spin is so captivating that people follow them.

Frankfurt wrote a very short book, *On Bullshit*, that is easy for one to understand, and he contributed to the attention to philosophy with his work. He also wrote four other books intended for the mainstream reader in America.

CHAPTER 37: SAM HARRIS

What I will do next and why remains at bottom a mystery, one that is fully determined by the laws of nature and the prior state of the universe.

Should we blame criminals for the crimes they commit?

Sam Harris grew up in Los Angeles to a Jewish other and Quaker father. While not brought up with any attention to religion, Harris had always been interested in religion. He attended Stanford University with a major in English, but he left in his sophomore year to travel to Asia and study meditation with Hindu and Buddhist teachers. He then returned to Stanford and earned a BA in philosophy and a PhD in neuroscience at the University of California. He has written four books, and he is cofounder of Project Reason, a nonprofit foundation that spreads scientific knowledge and secular values.

Harris wrote a book telling of a horrific crime where two men robbed, raped, and then killed a family, except the father, by burning the house down. When the police asked the criminal why he did not untie the family, he replied that he had not thought of it. Harris comments that we do not care about the horrible childhoods the criminals had experienced, and that if he had the same genes, life history, brain, and soul of the man, he would have done the same thing. He bases this belief on neuroscience, which shows that the decision to do something is made in the brain before we consciously decide to do it. We believe we have free will, but our actions are a result of our thoughts, which are a result of our brain's physiology and states.

We cannot decide what we will think next; it just happens. Consciousness just appears, we have no control over it. How we can hold people responsible for their actions is a concern of Harris. If we are just a result of our biology, as he believes, our entire criminal justice system is faulty. He agrees that we should isolate those who are at risk for harming others, but we cannot blame them.

Harris feels that our desires come from the cosmos. Our intentions tell about us, but we do not understand the source of intentions. He says that we make up reasons for what we decide to do after the fact, and free will is an illusion. He believes that the idea of free will comes from religion.

CHAPTER 38:
JULIAN BAGGINI

The idea of the self as a construction is one that many want to resist, because it seems to imply that it is not real. But of course constructions can be perfectly real.

You, the person, is not separate from these thoughts, the thing having them. Rather you are just the collection of these thoughts.

Baggini observes that an adult is the same person that he was as a child. He raises the questions that if an adult has no memories from his childhood, is he still himself? Is a transgendered person still the same? Is a person with dementia still the same? Is the concept of me a function of the mind or the body?

Baggini contrasts the "pearl" view of self with the "personhood" view of self. The pearl view says that regardless of how much we change, we still have the essence of ourselves, so we are the same person. The pearl view says that we have free will and may even 'live' on after our physical death. Neuroscience, however, has not found any evidence of this pearl in any part of the brain. We have a sense of self over time, an autobiographical self that remembers vivid stories of our past. We have a sense of who we are, and even if people have brain injury, they maintain that sense of self.

Baggini maintains that if there is no

source or spot of self in the brain, character does not exist either. One's environment has a much greater impact on what we do than any facet of our mind or body, and human dignity and character are not real. He believes many people live good lives simply because circumstances have not tested them. We are who we are because of our social environment, family, and friends because we take on their view of the world. We influence others and they influence us. We are defined more by our relationships with others than by our memories, he asserts.

Buddhists believe that we have no fixed essence; instead, we are a sum of our thoughts and experiences, and this combination creates a self, a self that has different facets. Baggini believes that we can live a meaningful life by fully experiencing all of our facets.

Baggini received a PhD in philosophy, and he studied personal identity specifically. He is the author of five books, including *The Ethics Toolkit*.

PART II
PHILOSOPHIES

These major schools of thought, or philosophies, are listed alphabetically.

Absurdism

You will never be happy if you continue to search for what happiness consists of. You will never live if you are looking for the meaning of life. – Albert Camus (1913-1960)

Absurdism is a philosophy stating that the efforts of humanity to find meaning in the universe will fail, so such efforts are absurd because no meaning exists. Absurdism suggests that even if meaning exists, the pursuit of it is not important. It is different from nihilism by its subjective view of humanity, theology and meaning. It is similar to existentialism. Soren Kierkegaard wrote on absurdism, and Albert Camus is associated with it as well.

Behaviorism

Give me a dozen healthy infants, well-formed, and my own specified world to bring them up in and I'll guarantee to take any one at random and train him to become any type of specialist I might select--doctor, lawyer, artist, merchant-chief, and, yes, even beggarman and thief, regardless of his talents, penchants, tendencies, abilities, vocations, and race of his ancestors. I am going beyond my facts and I admit it, but so have the advocates of the contrary and they have been doing it for many thousands of years.- **John B. Watson**

Behaviorism is a philosophical theory that branched off into psychology, as psychology was formed as a separate science. Behaviorism is based on the belief that organisms are the product of their conditioning or environment, rather than a product of their heredity or choices. It is a purely objective experimental branch of natural science whose theoretical goal is the prediction and control of behavior. Introspection and interpretation of information do not play any part in behaviorism.

The behaviorists include B.F. Skinner, Watson, and Bandura. Behaviorists believe in clearly defining behavior and measuring changes in behavior. They look for explanations for human behavior. Behaviorism, therefore, looks for simple explanations of human behavior from a very scientific standpoint.

Deontology

Morality is not properly the doctrine of how we may make ourselves happy, but how we can make ourselves worthy of being happy. - Kant

Deontology is a theory of ethics that states the purpose of ethics is to bind you to your duty, and that duty is not dependent on consequences. You are duty bound to keep your word and do your duty whether it is pleasant or beneficial. One type of deontology is the Divine Command theory, which states that a law is morally binding because God commands it. Kant's rationalism is another type of deontology.

Determinism

Everything is determined, the beginning as well as the end, by forces over which we have no control. It is determined for the insect as well as the star. Human beings, vegetables, or cosmic dust, we all dance to a mysterious tune, intoned in the distance by an invisible piper. – Albert Einstein (1879-1955)

Determinism is the philosophical theory that every event, including human thought, behavior, decision and action, is determined by a sequence of prior events. Determinists generally believe in causal determinism, believing that there is only one possible outcome for that sequence of events, and deny that humans lack free will. All events have a cause and effect and the precise combination of events at a particular time results in a particular outcome.

Another subgroup of determinism is theological determinism, which asserts that one's future is predetermined by God. Either God know actions humans will take in advance by omniscience, or He predetermines those actions.

Environmental determinism, also called Climatic or Geographical determinism, says that all human and cultural development is determined by environment, climate and geography, rather than society.

Logical Determinism is the idea that all statements, whether about the past, present or future, are either true or false. The question then arises as to how choices can be free, given that what one does in the future is already determined as true or false in the present.

Biological Determinism is the idea that all actions, beliefs, and desires are fixed by our genetic make-up and chemistry and cannot be changed.

Emergentism , also called Generativism, states that free will does not exist although it appears that free will exists because of the great variety of behavior. The unpredictability of emerging behavior that we see in daily life actually comes from complex, but deterministic, processes.

Dualism

There is a dualism inherent in democracy-- opposing forces pushing against each other, always. Culture clashes. Different belief systems. All coming together to create this country. But this balance takes a great deal of energy. -Libba Bray

Dualism is the philosophy of mind that emphasizes the separateness of mind and matter. Dualism denies that the mind is the same as the brain, and some deny that the mind is wholly a product of the brain.

Substance dualists argue that the mind

and the body are composed of different substances. The mind is a thinking thing that lacks the usual attributes of physical objects, like size, shape, and location. Interactionists believe that minds and bodies causally affect one another. Other types of dualists assert that bodily events can have mental events as effects. Property dualists argue that mental states come from brain states.

Empiricism

At issue is not only knowledge of the world but our survival as individuals and as a species. All the basic technologies ever invented by humans to feed and protect themselves depend on a relentless commitment to hard-nosed empiricism: you cannot assume that your arrowheads will pierce the hide of a bison or that your raft will float just because the omens are propitious and you have been given supernatural reassurance that they will. You have to be sure. -Barbara Ehrenreich

Empiricism is the philosophical idea that one can find what is true or correct based on data and facts. Anyone can refute that data or validate it using his on senses. It is in opposition to the belief that one can know the truth by faith. Empiricism is an important part of the scientific method because theories and hypotheses must be observed and tested to be considered accurate. Empiricists tend to doubt that anything can be known for sure, and they tend not to believe in absolute truths.

Empiricists believe that one's knowledge of the world is based on experiences, particularly sensory experiences. According to empiricists, learning is based on our observations and perception, the way that we process observations. Therefore, knowledge is not possible without experience.

Epicureanism

Do not spoil what you have by desiring what you have not; remember that what you now have was once among the things you only hoped for. – Epicurus (341-270 BC)

Epicureanism is a philosophy based on the belief that life's highest good is pleasure, being free from distress and pain. The word later took on the connotation of living a life of sensual pleasure, luxury, and specifically, indulging in gourmet food. Epicureans are skeptical of superstition and divinity.

Existentialism

Be that self which one truly is. – Soren Kierkegaard (1813-1855)

Existentialism is the philosophical movement that proposes that individual human beings create the meaning and essence of their lives as persons. Human beings are to make their own choices in life and find their own meaning, with or without

God. Existential philosophers range from the religious like Kierkegaard to the anti-religious like Nietzsche.

It is a philosophical outlook that centers on the concepts of freedom and choice. Believing that man has no preordained reason or purpose from a Higher Power, Existentialists assert that man must develop his own purpose and way to impact his world.

Idealism

You see, idealism detached from action is just a dream. But idealism allied with pragmatism, with rolling up your sleeves and making the world bend a bit, is very exciting. It's very real. It's very strong.

Bono

Idealism is a descriptor of any philosophy based on the belief that there is a spiritual truth that can be sought. It is in opposition to the belief that man can only find truth through what he gathers from the senses. It says that there is a difference between the appearance of something and the thing itself.

Kant and Hegel were both idealists.

Intuitionism

There are moral truths that come to be self-evident to us just as mathematical axioms do,
-W.D Ross

Intuitionism is the belief that reason is

not the source of basic ethical truths, and neither are feelings. Ethical beliefs come from a special power, man's intuition. Some intuitionists believe that this special power of intuition is implanted in us by God, and others believe it comes from other sources. Wherever it comes from, intuitionists believe that this is a power we all have, and if we are receptive to it and honest about it, we cannot deny its existence. When you have a genuine intuition of rightness or wrongness, you cannot help but know that it is a universal ethical truth. Philosophers debate if we intuit general properties or a certain number of ethical truths, and sometimes intuited ethics conflict, but the greatest duty overrides the smallest, according to a major intuitionist philosopher, W.D. Ross.

Materialism

There is no such thing as material covetousness. All covetousness is spiritual. ...Any so-called material thing that you want is merely a symbol: you want it not for itself, but because it will content your spirit for the moment. - **Mark Twain**

Materialism is the belief that truth is only what is real and can be seen and experienced. It proposes that there is no spirit or consciousness. There is no room for faith in the world. It states that everything in the universe is matter, without any true spiritual or intellectual existence. Materialism can also refer to a doctrine that material success and progress are the highest values in life. Materialism asserts that the universe is mechanical and that it runs by natural laws, unaffected by any supreme power or what man does.

Dialectical Materialism is the philosophical basis of Marxism and Communism. It states that any statement and its opposite can be reconciled, and it can be applied to economics and other fields. Marx asserts that in order for human beings to survive they need to produce the material goods for life, and this production should be through a division of labor. It is the cornerstone of Communism.

Naturalism

Naturalism is the view that the physical world is a self-contained system that works by blind, unbroken natural laws. Naturalism doesn't come right out and say there's nothing beyond nature. Rather, it says that nothing beyond nature could have any conceivable relevance to what happens in nature. Naturalism's answer to theism is not atheism but benign neglect. People are welcome to believe in God, though not a God who makes a difference in the natural order. - William A. Dembski

Naturalism is the belief that the universe runs according to physical laws and there is no truth beyond the physical universe. The physical realm is the only part of the world that matters. It denies the existence of God, for the most part, and believes that there is no supreme being who intervenes in the world.

Nihilism

Man hands on misery to man. It deepens like a coastal shelf. Get out as early as you can, And don't have any kids yourself. – Philip Larkin (1922-1985)

Nihilism is a philosophy that assets that life is without objective meaning, purpose, value or truth. Proponents of Nihilism reject belief in a higher creator, and life is pointless. Nihilism is often associated with pessimism, depression and immorality. Many artistic movements have been associated with nihilism, such as Dadaism, Futurism and Surrealism.

Nominalism

The menu is not the meal. -Alan W. Watts

Nominalism is the doctrine that abstract concepts, general terms or universals have no independent existence but exist only as names. Therefore, various objects labelled by the same term have nothing in common but their name. Put another way, only actual physical particulars are real, and universals exist only subsequent to particular things, being just verbal abstractions.

Objectivism

Man has been called a rational being, but rationality is a matter of choice – and the alternative his nature offers him is: rational being or suicidal animal. Man has to be man – by choice; he has to hold his life as a value — by choice; he has to learn to sustain it – by choice; he has to discover the values it requires and practice his virtues – by choice. – Ayn Rand (1905-1982)

Objectivism is a philosophy developed by Ayn Rand. It states that there is a reality that is independent of the mind, and that individuals are in contact with this reality through the senses and one's perception. She believed that human beings gain this objective knowledge from perception by measurement and form valid concepts based on these perceptions. Objectivism claims that the meaning of life is the pursuit of one's own happiness or "rational self-interest," and that the only social system consistent with this morality is one with full respect for individual rights, embodied in pure, consensual laissez-faire capitalism, or libertarianism.

Positivism

The deepest sin against the human mind is to believe things without evidence. – Thomas H. Huxley (1825-1895)

Positivism is a philosophy that states that the only authentic knowledge is scientific knowledge that can only come from affirming theories through the scientific method. It is closely associated with empiricism and rationalism. It was first theorized by Auguste Comte in the mid-19th century, and developed into a modern philosophy.

Postmodernism

From my perspective, 'postmodernism' merely names an interesting set of developments in the social order that is based on the presumption that God does not matter.-
Stanley Hauerwas

Postmodernism is an outlook based on awareness of stories and assumptions that shape the world, such as "progress" and "success." The heart of postmodernism is the view that reality *cannot* be known or described objectively. This contrasts to the modernist view that says reality *can* be understood objectively. It is a philosophical idea that also describes the arts, meaning an openness to meaning and authority from unexpected places. There is a willingness to borrow from other philosophies and traditions, and to create a patchwork quilt of ideas to accept. There is no Truth, just truths, according to postmodernism.

Poststructuralism

Oddly, the last people in the humanities who are still talking about 'absolute truth' are the Post-Structuralists in the business of demolishing it" - Alan Bilton.

Poststructuralism is a philosophy that is similar to post-modernism, but different. It applies most specifically to writing and texts. It states that the reader is more important than the author and what the reader thinks is more important than the intended theme. The culture and society of the reader is just as critical as the text itself. Poststructuralism suggests that readers refute the ideas found in texts, allowing for multiple text interpretations. Objective truth is unimportant; it is interpretation that matters.

Pragmatism

It's really easy to have a nice philosophy about openness, but moving the world in that direction is a different thing. It requires both understanding where you want to go and being pragmatic about getting there. Mark Zuckerberg

Pragmatism is the philosophical approach that focuses on the end, rather than the beginning or the process of thought. The value of the idea is whether it works to benefit the user or believer. Pragmatists are those who claim that an ideology is true if it works well. They state that the acceptance of a view is found in learning that it works. If it is not practical, it should be rejected, according to this view. Famous pragmatists are William James and John Dewey. Pragmatism began in the United States. It has affected many other social sciences as well as philosophy.

Rationalism

Rationalism, which is the feeling that everything is subject to and completely explicable by Reason, consequently rejects everything not visible and calculable. Francis Parker   Yockey

Rationalism is the belief that truth or

knowledge can only be found through reason, rather than through the senses or faith. Thought is more important than observation in determining reality. The most commonly discussed difference between rationalists and empiricists concerns the question of the source of ideas. Rationalists tend to think that some ideas, such as the idea of God, are innate, where empiricists believe that all ideas come from experience. Although the rationalists tend to be remembered for their positive beliefs concerning innate ideas, they also believe that all ideas cannot be accounted for on the basis of experience alone.

Realism

There is an interesting scientific dispute about realism and optimism. Some find that very optimistic people have benign illusions about themselves. These people may think they have more control, or more skill, than they actually do. Others have found that optimistic people have a good handle on reality. The jury is still out. - Martin Seligman

If there are moral facts, how can we know them? For a realist, moral facts are as certain as mathematical facts. Moral facts and mathematical facts are abstract and are different from natural facts. One cannot see moral facts as one could see a plant. These limitations do not stop realists from disagreeing on moral practices based on moral facts.

Realism in literature is depicting events and the world as they really are, rather than presenting them ideally or romantically.

Relativism

Having a clear faith, based on the creed of the church is often labeled today as fundamentalism. Whereas relativism, which is letting oneself be tossed and swept along by every wind of teaching, look like the only attitude acceptable to today's standards. Pope Benedict   XVI

Relativism is the philosophical view that every belief is equally valid, and that all truth depends on the views of the individual. Therefore, all morality, all religions, and all political movements are truth to the individual who accepts them. There are various types of relativism. One type is cognitive relativism, which refers to truth. Cognitive relativism asserts that all truth is based on the individual, with the premise that no system of truth is more valid than another one, and that there is no objective standard of truth. It rejects the idea that there is a God of absolute truth. Another type is moral/ethical relativism, which asserts that all morals are relative to the social group that creates that moral standard. A third is situational relativism, which promotes flexibility and proposes that the ethics of a situation, right or wrong actions, are dependent upon the situation.

The philosophy of relativism is pervasive in our culture today, with the rejection of God and absolute truth. However, all views are not readily accepted, and one who rejects the philosophy of moral relativism and its "tolerance" philosophy is labeled as intolerant. Ironically, it is hypocritical that those who profess that all points of view are true reject those who profess absolutes in morality

Statement that reflect a philosophy of relativism are as follows: "It is true for you, but not for me;" and "It may have been wrong to do it yesterday, but today the situation is different, so it is okay to do it."

Secular Humanism

There is not sufficient love and goodness in the world to permit us to give some of it away to imaginary beings. – Friedrich Nietzsche (1844-1900)

Secular Humanism is an atheistic philosophy that upholds reason, ethics and justice as the principles of life. It rejects the concept of a supernatural creator, and says that the meaning of life is to be found purely in human terms. It upholds that there is no absolute truth or absolute morality, and that truth, meaning and morality are unique to each person. Adherents to secular humanism include Friedrich Nietzsche, Bertrand Russell and Richard Dawkins.

Solipsism

Nothing exists; Even if something exists, nothing can be known about it; Even if something could be known about it, knowledge about it can't be communicated to others. Gorgias (485-375 BC)

Solipsism is the idea that one can only know that self exists and that anything else cannot be known to exist. Solipsists place emphasis on what is subjective, and that what we perceive to be true for one person may not be true for another. Proponents are Greek pre-Socratic philosopher Gorgias, Plato, and Descartes. Solipsism is often associated with nihilism and materialism.

Stoicism

The basic philosophy of stoicism is that you have nothing real external to your own consciousness, that the only thing real is in fact your consciousness. Roger Avary

Stoicism is a philosophy that emphasizes calmness and peace in the face of life's ups and downs. The philosophy supports the search for and attainment of virtue. It proposes that the path to happiness is aligning one's actions with fate or universal will. Stoicism was one of the most important and enduring philosophies to emerge from the Greek and Roman world, one that created theories of mind. The Stoics believed that the mind is representative of that all mental states and acts. The senses take in information, which is then processed and placed into a logical organization. They believed that the soul is unified and that all the faculties are rational, and they concluded that the passions are the result, not of irrationality, but of errors in judgement.

Structuralism

"I studied Comparative Literature at Cornell. Structuralism was real big then. The idea of reading and writing as being this

language game. There's a lot of appeal to that. It's nice to think of it as this playful kind of thing. But I think that another way to look at it is "Look, I just want to be sincere. I want to write something and make you feel something and maybe you will go out and do something." And it seems that the world is in such bad shape now that we don't have time to do nothing but language games. That's how it seems to me."

- William T. Vollmann

Structuralism is the view that human beings can only be understood in the framework of society and social institutions. Linguistics, sociology, anthropology and other fields attempt to analyze their field into a complex system of interrelated parts. Structuralism suggests that all beliefs, actions, and morals of humans, even perception and thought itself, are not natural, but constructed using our language system.

Structuralism is based on four ideas: every system has a structure; the structure determines the position of each element; structural laws deal with interrelationships between concepts; and structures are what lie beneath the surface of meaning.

Theological voluntarism

Do the gods love piety because it is pious, or is it pious because they love it? -Plato

Theological voluntarism is a form of absolutism that states that moral principles are set by God, God commands them, and God does not change or make exceptions. God's standards are fixed, absolute, and eternal. What is right is whatever God commands or whatever God chooses. God does not condemn murder because it is wrong; murder is wrong because God condemns it. The belief that what God wills is ethical. Also called the Divine Command theory of ethics, this theory says that only what God commands is good.

Transcendentalism

The theory of books is noble. The scholar of

the first age received into him the world

around; brooded thereon; gave it the new

arrangement of his own mind, and uttered it

again.

It came into him, life; it went out from him,

truth.

It came to him, short-lived actions; it went out

from him, immortal thoughts.

It came to him, business; it went from him,

poetry.

It was dead fact; now, it is quick thought.

It can stand, and it can go.

It now endures, it now flies, it now inspires

Precisely in proportion to the depth of mind

from which it issued, so high does it soar, so

long does it sing.

-Ralph Waldo Emerson

Transcendentalism,   labelled   an

"American" philosophy describes a simple idea, namely that people have knowledge about themselves and the world around them that "transcends" or goes beyond what they can see, hear, taste, touch or feel. This knowledge comes through intuition and imagination, not through logic or the senses. People can trust themselves to be their own authority on what is right. A transcendentalist is a person who accepts these ideas, not as religious beliefs, but as a way of understanding life relationships.

The individuals most closely associated with transcendentalism are Ralph Waldo Emerson, Nathaniel Hawthorne, Longfellow, and Henry David Thoreau.

Utilitarianism

It is better to be a human being dissatisfied, than a pig satisfied; better to be Socrates dissatisfied than a fool satisfied. – John Stuart Mill (1806-1873)

Utilitarianism is a philosophy that believes that achieving the greatest happiness or welfare for the greatest number of people is the goal of one's life. It is representative of the ethical doctrine that the moral worth of an action depends on its contribution and use. It is a form of consequentialism, meaning that the moral worth of an action is determined by its outcome, that is the ends justify the means. Utilitarianism was first theorized by Jeremy Bentham who declared that 'good' was whatever brought the greatest happiness to the greatest number of people. However, the philosophy is most associated with John Stuart Mill and his book Utilitarianism (1863).

III. PHILOSOPHY IN THE WORDS OF FOUR MAJOR PHILOSOPHERS

Brief Portions of Important Works of Aristotle, St. Thomas Aquinas, Descartes, and Plato

Categories by Aristotle

1

Things are said to be named 'equivocally' when, though they have a common name, the definition corresponding with the name differs for each. Thus, a real man and a figure in a picture can both lay claim to the name 'animal'; yet these are equivocally so named, for, though they have a common name, the definition corresponding with the name differs for each. For should any one define in what sense each is an animal, his definition in the one case will be appropriate to that case only.

On the other hand, things are said to be named 'univocally' which have both the name and the definition answering to the name in common. A man and an ox are both 'animal', and these are univocally so named, inasmuch as not only the name, but also the definition, is the same in both cases: for if a man should state in what sense each is an animal, the statement in the one case would be identical with that in the other.

Things are said to be named 'derivatively', which derive their name from some other name, but differ from it in termination. Thus the grammarian derives his name from the word 'grammar', and the courageous man from the word 'courage'.

2

Forms of speech are either simple or composite. Examples of the latter are such expressions as 'the man runs', 'the man wins'; of the former 'man', 'ox', 'runs', 'wins'.

Of things themselves some are predicable of a subject, and are never present in a subject. Thus 'man' is predicable of the individual man, and is never present in a subject.

By being 'present in a subject' I do not mean present as parts are present in a whole, but being incapable of existence apart from the said subject.

Some things, again, are present in a subject, but are never predicable of a subject. For instance, a certain point of grammatical knowledge is present in the mind, but is not predicable of any subject; or again, a certain whiteness may be present in the body (for colour requires a material basis), yet it is never predicable of anything.

Other things, again, are both predicable of a subject and present in a subject. Thus while knowledge is present in the human mind, it is predicable of grammar.

There is, lastly, a class of things which are neither present in a subject nor predicable of a subject, such as the individual man or the individual horse. But, to speak more generally, that which is individual and has the character of a unit is never predicable of a subject. Yet in some cases there is nothing to prevent such being present in a subject. Thus a certain point of grammatical knowledge is present in a subject.

3

When one thing is predicated of another, all that which is predicable of the predicate will be predicable also of the subject. Thus, 'man' is predicated of the individual man; but 'animal' is predicated of 'man'; it will, therefore, be predicable of the individual man also: for the individual man is both 'man' and 'animal'.

If genera are different and co-ordinate, their differentiae are themselves different in kind. Take as an instance the genus 'animal' and the genus 'knowledge'. 'With feet', 'two-footed', 'winged', 'aquatic', are differentiae of 'animal'; the species of knowledge are not distinguished by the same differentiae. One species of knowledge does not differ from another in being 'two-footed'.

But where one genus is subordinate to another, there is nothing to prevent their having the same differentiae: for the greater class is predicated of the lesser, so that all the differentiae of the predicate will be differentiae also of the subject.

4

Expressions which are in no way composite signify substance, quantity, quality, relation, place, time, position, state, action, or affection. To sketch my meaning roughly, examples of substance are 'man' or 'the horse', of quantity, such terms as 'two cubits long' or 'three cubits long', of quality, such attributes as 'white', 'grammatical'. 'Double', 'half', 'greater', fall under the category of relation; 'in a the market place', 'in the Lyceum', under that of place; 'yesterday', 'last year', under that of time. 'Lying', 'sitting', are terms indicating position, 'shod', 'armed', state; 'to lance', 'to cauterize', action; 'to be lanced', 'to be cauterized', affection.

No one of these terms, in and by itself, involves an affirmation; it is by the combination of such terms that positive or negative statements arise. For every assertion must, as is admitted, be either true or false, whereas expressions which are not in any way composite such as 'man', 'white', 'runs', 'wins', cannot be either true or false.

5

Substance, in the truest and primary and most definite sense of the word, is that which is neither predicable of a subject nor present in a subject; for instance, the individual man or horse. But in a secondary sense those things are called substances within which, as species, the primary substances are included; also those which, as genera, include the species. For instance, the individual man is included in the species 'man', and the genus to which the species belongs is 'animal'; these, therefore-that is to say, the species 'man' and the genus 'animal,-are termed secondary substances.

It is plain from what has been said that both the name and the definition of the predicate must be predicable of the subject. For instance, 'man' is predicted of the individual man. Now in this case the name of the species man' is applied to the individual, for we use the term 'man' in describing the individual; and the definition of 'man' will also be predicated of the individual man, for the individual man is both man and animal. Thus, both the name and the definition of the species are predicable of the individual.

With regard, on the other hand, to those things which are present in a subject, it is generally the case that neither their name nor their definition is predicable of that in which they are present. Though, however, the definition is never predicable, there is nothing in certain cases to prevent the name being used. For instance, 'white' being present in a body is predicated of that in which it is present, for a body is called white: the definition, however, of the colour white' is never predicable of the body.

Everything except primary substances is either predicable of a primary substance or present in a primary substance. This becomes evident by reference to particular instances which occur. 'Animal' is predicated of the species 'man', therefore of the individual man, for if there were no individual man of whom it could be predicated, it could not be predicated of the species 'man' at all. Again, colour is present in body, therefore in individual bodies, for if there were no individual body in which it was present, it could not be present in body at all. Thus everything except primary substances is either predicated of primary substances, or is present in them, and if these last did not exist, it would be impossible for anything else to exist.

Of secondary substances, the species is more truly substance than the genus, being more nearly related to primary substance. For if any one should render an account of what a primary substance is, he would render a more instructive account, and one more proper to the subject, by stating the species than by stating the genus. Thus, he would give a more instructive account of an individual man by stating that he was man than by stating that he was animal, for the former description is peculiar to the individual in a greater degree, while the latter is too general. Again, the man who gives an account of the nature of an individual tree will give a more instructive account by mentioning the species 'tree' than by mentioning the genus 'plant'.

Moreover, primary substances are most properly called substances in virtue of the fact that they are the entities which underlie everything else, and that everything else is either predicated of them or present in them. Now the same relation which subsists between primary substance and everything else subsists also between the species and the genus: for the species is to the genus as subject is to predicate, since the genus is predicated of the species, whereas the species cannot be predicated of the genus. Thus we have a second ground for asserting that the species is more truly substance than the genus.

Of species themselves, except in the case of such as are genera, no one is more truly substance than another. We should not give a more appropriate account of the individual man by stating the species to which he belonged, than we should of an individual horse by adopting the same method of definition. In the same way, of primary substances, no one is more truly substance than another; an individual man is not more truly substance than an individual ox.

It is, then, with good reason that of all that remains, when we exclude primary substances, we concede to species and genera alone the name 'secondary substance', for these alone of all the predicates convey a knowledge of primary substance. For it is by stating the species or the genus that we appropriately define any individual man; and we shall make our definition more exact by stating the former than by stating the latter. All other things that we state, such as that he is white, that he runs, and so on, are irrelevant to the definition. Thus it is just that these alone, apart from primary substances, should be called substances.

Further, primary substances are most properly so called, because they underlie and are the subjects of everything else. Now the same relation that subsists between primary substance and everything else subsists also between the species and the genus to which the primary substance belongs, on the one hand, and every attribute which is not included within these, on the other. For these are the subjects of all such. If we call an individual man 'skilled in grammar', the predicate is applicable also to the species and to the genus to which he belongs. This law holds good in all cases.

It is a common characteristic of all substance that it is never present in a subject. For primary substance is neither present in a subject nor predicated of a subject; while, with regard to secondary substances, it is clear from the following arguments (apart from others) that they are not present in a subject. For 'man' is predicated of the individual man, but is not present in any subject: for manhood is not present in the individual man. In the same way, 'animal' is also predicated of the individual man, but is not present in him. Again, when a thing is present in a subject, though the name may quite well be applied to that in which it is present, the definition cannot be applied. Yet of secondary substances, not only the name, but also the definition, applies to the subject: we should use both the definition of the species and that of the genus with reference to the individual man. Thus substance cannot be present in a subject.

Yet this is not peculiar to substance, for

it is also the case that differentiae cannot be present in subjects. The characteristics 'terrestrial' and 'two-footed' are predicated of the species 'man', but not present in it. For they are not in man. Moreover, the definition of the differentia may be predicated of that of which the differentia itself is predicated. For instance, if the characteristic 'terrestrial' is predicated of the species 'man', the definition also of that characteristic may be used to form the predicate of the species 'man': for 'man' is terrestrial.

The fact that the parts of substances appear to be present in the whole, as in a subject, should not make us apprehensive lest we should have to admit that such parts are not substances: for in explaining the phrase 'being present in a subject', we stated' that we meant 'otherwise than as parts in a whole'.

It is the mark of substances and of

differentiae that, in all propositions of which they form the predicate, they are predicated univocally. For all such propositions have for their subject either the individual or the species. It is true that, inasmuch as primary substance is not predicable of anything, it can never form the predicate of any proposition. But of secondary substances, the species is predicated of the individual, the genus both of the species and of the individual. Similarly the differentiae are predicated of the species and of the individuals. Moreover, the definition of the species and that of the genus are applicable to the primary substance, and that of the genus to the species. For all that is predicated of the predicate will be predicated also of the subject. Similarly, the definition of the differentiae will be applicable to the species and to the individuals. But it was stated above that the word 'univocal' was applied to those things which had both name and definition in common. It is, therefore, established that in every proposition, of which either substance or a differentia forms the predicate, these are predicated univocally.

All substance appears to signify that which is individual. In the case of primary substance this is indisputably true, for the thing is a unit. In the case of secondary substances, when we speak, for instance, of 'man' or 'animal', our form of speech gives the impression that we are here also indicating that which is individual, but the impression is not strictly true; for a secondary substance is not an individual, but a class with a certain qualification; for it is not one and single as a primary substance is; the words 'man', 'animal', are predicable of more than one subject.

Yet species and genus do not merely

indicate quality, like the term 'white'; 'white' indicates quality and nothing further, but species and genus determine the quality with reference to a substance: they signify substance qualitatively differentiated. The determinate qualification covers a larger field in the case of the genus that in that of the species: he who uses the word 'animal' is herein using a word of wider extension than he who uses the word 'man'.

Another mark of substance is that it has no contrary. What could be the contrary of any primary substance, such as the individual man or animal? It has none. Nor can the species or the genus have a contrary. Yet this characteristic is not peculiar to substance, but is true of many other things, such as quantity. There is nothing that forms the contrary of 'two cubits long' or of 'three cubits long', or of 'ten', or of any such term. A man may contend that 'much' is the contrary of 'little', or 'great' of 'small', but of definite quantitative terms no contrary exists.

Substance, again, does not appear to admit of variation of degree. I do not mean by this that one substance cannot be more or less truly substance than another, for it has already been stated' that this is the case; but that no single substance admits of varying degrees within itself. For instance, one particular substance, 'man', cannot be more or less man either than himself at some other time or than some other man. One man cannot be more man than another, as that which is white may be more or less white than some other white object, or as that which is beautiful may be more or less beautiful than some other beautiful object. The same quality, moreover, is said to subsist in a thing in varying degrees at different times. A body, being white, is said to be whiter at one time than it was before, or, being warm, is said to be warmer or less warm than at some other time. But substance is not said to be more or less that which it is: a man is not more truly a man at one time than he was before, nor is anything, if it is substance, more or less what it is. Substance, then, does not admit of variation of degree.

The most distinctive mark of substance appears to be that, while remaining numerically one and the same, it is capable of admitting contrary qualities. From among things other than substance, we should find ourselves unable to bring forward any which possessed this mark. Thus, one and the same colour cannot be white and black. Nor can the same one action be good and bad: this law holds good with everything that is not substance. But one and the selfsame substance, while retaining its identity, is yet capable of admitting contrary qualities. The same individual person is at one time white, at another black, at one time warm, at another cold, at one time good, at another bad. This capacity is found nowhere else, though it might be maintained that a statement or opinion was an exception to the rule. The same statement, it is agreed, can be both true and false. For if the statement 'he is sitting' is true, yet, when the person in question has risen, the same statement will be false. The same applies to opinions. For if any one thinks truly that a person is sitting, yet, when that person has risen, this same opinion, if still held, will be false. Yet although this exception may be allowed, there is, nevertheless, a difference in the manner in which the thing takes place. It is by themselves changing that substances admit contrary qualities. It is thus that that which was hot becomes cold, for it has entered into a different state. Similarly that which was white becomes black, and that which was bad good, by a process of change; and in the same way in all other cases it is by changing that substances are capable of admitting contrary qualities. But statements and opinions themselves remain unaltered in all respects: it is by the alteration in the facts of the case that the contrary quality comes to be theirs. The statement 'he is sitting' remains unaltered, but it is at one time true, at another false, according to circumstances. What has been said of statements applies also to opinions. Thus, in respect of the manner in which the thing takes place, it is the peculiar mark of substance that it should be capable of admitting contrary qualities; for it is by itself changing that it does so.

If, then, a man should make this exception and contend that statements and opinions are capable of admitting contrary qualities, his contention is unsound. For statements and opinions are said to have this capacity, not because they themselves undergo modification, but because this modification occurs in the case of something else. The truth or falsity of a statement depends on facts, and not on any power on the part of the statement itself of admitting contrary qualities. In short, there is nothing which can alter the nature of statements and opinions. As, then, no change takes place in themselves, these cannot be said to be capable of admitting contrary qualities.

But it is by reason of the modification which takes place within the substance itself that a substance is said to be capable of admitting contrary qualities; for a substance admits within itself either disease or health, whiteness or blackness. It is in this sense that it is said to be capable of admitting contrary qualities.

To sum up, it is a distinctive mark of substance, that, while remaining numerically one and the same, it is capable of admitting contrary qualities, the modification taking place through a change in the substance itself.

Let these remarks suffice on the subject of substance.

6

Quantity is either discrete or continuous. Moreover, some quantities are such that each part of the whole has a relative position to the other parts: others have within them no such relation of part to part.

Instances of discrete quantities are number and speech; of continuous, lines, surfaces, solids, and, besides these, time and place.

In the case of the parts of a number, there is no common boundary at which they join. For example: two fives make ten, but the two fives have no common boundary, but are separate; the parts three and seven also do not join at any boundary. Nor, to generalize, would it ever be possible in the case of number that there should be a common boundary among the parts; they are always separate. Number, therefore, is a discrete quantity.

The same is true of speech. That speech is a quantity is evident: for it is measured in long and short syllables. I mean here that speech which is vocal. Moreover, it is a discrete quantity for its parts have no common boundary. There is no common boundary at which the syllables join, but each is separate and distinct from the rest.

A line, on the other hand, is a continuous quantity, for it is possible to find a common boundary at which its parts join. In the case of the line, this common boundary is the point; in the case of the plane, it is the line: for the parts of the plane have also a common boundary. Similarly you can find a common boundary in the case of the parts of a solid, namely either a line or a plane.

Space and time also belong to this class of quantities. Time, past, present, and future, forms a continuous whole. Space, likewise, is a continuous quantity; for the parts of a solid occupy a certain space, and these have a common boundary; it follows that the parts of space also, which are occupied by the parts of the solid, have the same common boundary as the parts of the solid. Thus, not only time, but space also, is a continuous quantity, for its parts have a common boundary.

Quantities consist either of parts which bear a relative position each to each, or of parts which do not. The parts of a line bear a relative position to each other, for each lies somewhere, and it would be possible to distinguish each, and to state the position of each on the plane and to explain to what sort of part among the rest each was contiguous. Similarly the parts of a plane have position, for it could similarly be stated what was the position of each and what sort of parts were contiguous. The same is true with regard to the solid and to space. But it would be impossible to show that the arts of a number had a relative position each to each, or a particular position, or to state what parts were contiguous. Nor could this be done in the case of time, for none of the parts of time has an abiding existence, and that which does not abide can hardly have position. It would be better to say that such parts had a relative order, in virtue of one being prior to another. Similarly with number: in counting, 'one' is prior to 'two', and 'two' to 'three', and thus the parts of number may be said to possess a relative order, though it would be impossible to discover any distinct position for each. This holds good also in the case of speech. None of its parts has an abiding existence: when once a syllable is pronounced, it is not possible to retain it, so that, naturally, as the parts do not abide, they cannot have position. Thus, some quantities consist of parts which have position, and some of those which have not.

Strictly speaking, only the things which I have mentioned belong to the category of quantity: everything else that is called quantitative is a quantity in a secondary sense. It is because we have in mind some one of these quantities, properly so called, that we apply quantitative terms to other things. We speak of what is white as large, because the surface over which the white extends is large; we speak of an action or a process as lengthy, because the time covered is long; these things cannot in their own right claim the quantitative epithet. For instance, should any one explain how long an action was, his statement would be made in terms of the time taken, to the effect that it lasted a year, or something of that sort. In the same way, he would explain the size of a white object in terms of surface, for he would state the area which it covered. Thus the things already mentioned, and these alone, are in their intrinsic nature quantities; nothing else can claim the name in its own right, but, if at all, only in a secondary sense.

Quantities have no contraries. In the case of definite quantities this is obvious; thus, there is nothing that is the contrary of 'two cubits long' or of 'three cubits long', or of a surface, or of any such quantities. A man might, indeed, argue that 'much' was the contrary of 'little', and 'great' of 'small'. But these are not quantitative, but relative; things are not great or small absolutely, they are so called rather as the result of an act of comparison. For instance, a mountain is called small, a grain large, in virtue of the fact that the latter is greater than others of its kind, the former less. Thus there is a reference here to an external standard, for if the terms 'great' and 'small' were used absolutely, a mountain would never be called small or a grain large. Again, we say that there are many people in a village, and few in Athens, although those in the city are many times as numerous as those in the village: or we say that a house has many in it, and a theatre few, though those in the theatre far outnumber those in the house. The terms 'two cubits long, "three cubits long,' and so on indicate quantity, the terms 'great' and 'small' indicate relation, for they have reference to an external standard. It is, therefore, plain that these are to be classed as relative.

Again, whether we define them as quantitative or not, they have no contraries: for how can there be a contrary of an attribute which is not to be apprehended in or by itself, but only by reference to something external? Again, if 'great' and 'small' are contraries, it will come about that the same subject can admit contrary qualities at one and the same time, and that things will themselves be contrary to themselves. For it happens at times that the same thing is both small and great. For the same thing may be small in comparison with one thing, and great in comparison with another, so that the same thing comes to be both small and great at one and the same time, and is of such a nature as to admit contrary qualities at one and the same moment. Yet it was agreed, when substance was being discussed, that nothing admits contrary qualities at one and the same moment. For though substance is capable of admitting contrary qualities, yet no one is at the same time both sick and healthy, nothing is at the same time both white and black. Nor is there anything which is qualified in contrary ways at one and the same time.

Moreover, if these were contraries, they would themselves be contrary to themselves. For if 'great' is the contrary of 'small', and the same thing is both great and small at the same time, then 'small' or 'great' is the contrary of itself. But this is impossible. The term 'great', therefore, is not the contrary of the term 'small', nor 'much' of 'little'. And even though a man should call these terms not relative but quantitative, they would not have contraries.

It is in the case of space that quantity

most plausibly appears to admit of a contrary. For men define the term 'above' as the contrary of 'below', when it is the region at the centre they mean by 'below'; and this is so, because nothing is farther from the extremities of the universe than the region at the centre. Indeed, it seems that in defining contraries of every kind men have recourse to a spatial metaphor, for they say that those things are contraries which, within the same class, are separated by the greatest possible distance.

Quantity does not, it appears, admit of variation of degree. One thing cannot be two cubits long in a greater degree than another. Similarly with regard to number: what is 'three' is not more truly three than what is 'five' is five; nor is one set of three more truly three than another set. Again, one period of time is not said to be more truly time than another. Nor is there any other kind of quantity, of all that have been mentioned, with regard to which variation of degree can be predicated. The category of quantity, therefore, does not admit of variation of degree.

The most distinctive mark of quantity is that equality and inequality are predicated of it. Each of the aforesaid quantities is said to be equal or unequal. For instance, one solid is said to be equal or unequal to another; number, too, and time can have these terms applied to them, indeed can all those kinds of quantity that have been mentioned.

That which is not a quantity can by no means, it would seem, be termed equal or unequal to anything else. One particular disposition or one particular quality, such as whiteness, is by no means compared with another in terms of equality and inequality but rather in terms of similarity. Thus it is the distinctive mark of quantity that it can be called equal and unequal.

7

Those things are called relative, which, being either said to be of something else or related to something else, are explained by reference to that other thing. For instance, the word 'superior' is explained by reference to something else, for it is superiority over something else that is meant. Similarly, the expression 'double' has this external reference, for it is the double of something else that is meant. So it is with everything else of this kind. There are, moreover, other relatives, e.g. habit, disposition, perception, knowledge, and attitude. The significance of all these is explained by a reference to something else and in no other way. Thus, a habit is a habit of something, knowledge is knowledge of something, attitude is the attitude of something. So it is with all other relatives that have been mentioned. Those terms, then, are called relative, the nature of which is explained by reference to something else, the preposition 'of' or some other preposition being used to indicate the relation. Thus, one mountain is called great in comparison with son with another; for the mountain claims this attribute by comparison with something. Again, that which is called similar must be similar to something else, and all other such attributes have this external reference. It is to be noted that lying and standing and sitting are particular attitudes, but attitude is itself a relative term. To lie, to stand, to be seated, are not themselves attitudes, but take their name from the aforesaid attitudes.

It is possible for relatives to have contraries. Thus virtue has a contrary, vice, these both being relatives; knowledge, too, has a contrary, ignorance. But this is not the mark of all relatives; 'double' and 'triple' have no contrary, nor indeed has any such term.

It also appears that relatives can admit of variation of degree. For 'like' and 'unlike', 'equal' and 'unequal', have the modifications 'more' and 'less' applied to them, and each of these is relative in character: for the terms 'like' and 'unequal' bear 'unequal' bear a reference to something external. Yet, again, it is not every relative term that admits of variation of degree. No term such as 'double' admits of this modification. All relatives have correlatives: by the term 'slave' we mean the slave of a master, by the term 'master', the master of a slave; by 'double', the double of its hall; by 'half', the half of its double; by 'greater', greater than that which is less; by 'less,' less than that which is greater.

So it is with every other relative term;

but the case we use to express the correlation differs in some instances. Thus, by knowledge we mean knowledge the knowable; by the knowable, that which is to be apprehended by knowledge; by perception, perception of the perceptible; by the perceptible, that which is apprehended by perception.

Sometimes, however, reciprocity of correlation does not appear to exist. This comes about when a blunder is made, and that to which the relative is related is not accurately stated. If a man states that a wing is necessarily relative to a bird, the connexion between these two will not be reciprocal, for it will not be possible to say that a bird is a bird by reason of its wings. The reason is that the original statement was inaccurate, for the wing is not said to be relative to the bird qua bird, since many creatures besides birds have wings, but qua winged creature. If, then, the statement is made accurate, the connexion will be reciprocal, for we can speak of a wing, having reference necessarily to a winged creature, and of a winged creature as being such because of its wings.

Occasionally, perhaps, it is necessary to coin words, if no word exists by which a correlation can adequately be explained. If we define a rudder as necessarily having reference to a boat, our definition will not be appropriate, for the rudder does not have this reference to a boat qua boat, as there are boats which have no rudders. Thus we cannot use the terms reciprocally, for the word 'boat' cannot be said to find its explanation in the word 'rudder'. As there is no existing word, our definition would perhaps be more accurate if we coined some word like 'ruddered' as the correlative of 'rudder'. If we express ourselves thus accurately, at any rate the terms are reciprocally connected, for the 'ruddered' thing is 'ruddered' in virtue of its rudder. So it is in all other cases. A head will be more accurately defined as the correlative of that which is 'headed', than as that of an animal, for the animal does not have a head qua animal, since many animals have no head.

Thus we may perhaps most easily comprehend that to which a thing is related, when a name does not exist, if, from that which has a name, we derive a new name, and apply it to that with which the first is reciprocally connected, as in the aforesaid instances, when we derived the word 'winged' from 'wing' and from 'rudder'.

All relatives, then, if properly defined, have a correlative. I add this condition because, if that to which they are related is stated as haphazard and not accurately, the two are not found to be interdependent. Let me state what I mean more clearly. Even in the case of acknowledged correlatives, and where names exist for each, there will be no interdependence if one of the two is denoted, not by that name which expresses the correlative notion, but by one of irrelevant significance. The term 'slave,' if defined as related, not to a master, but to a man, or a biped, or anything of that sort, is not reciprocally connected with that in relation to which it is defined, for the statement is not exact. Further, if one thing is said to be correlative with another, and the terminology used is correct, then, though all irrelevant attributes should be removed, and only that one attribute left in virtue of which it was correctly stated to be correlative with that other, the stated correlation will still exist. If the correlative of 'the slave' is said to be 'the master', then, though all irrelevant attributes of the said 'master', such as 'biped', 'receptive of knowledge', 'human', should be removed, and the attribute 'master' alone left, the stated correlation existing between him and the slave will remain the same, for it is of a master that a slave is said to be the slave. On the other hand, if, of two correlatives, one is not correctly termed, then, when all other attributes are removed and that alone is left in virtue of which it was stated to be correlative, the stated correlation will be found to have disappeared.

For suppose the correlative of 'the slave' should be said to be 'the man', or the correlative of 'the wing"the bird'; if the attribute 'master' be withdrawn from' the man', the correlation between 'the man' and 'the slave' will cease to exist, for if the man is not a master, the slave is not a slave. Similarly, if the attribute 'winged' be withdrawn from 'the bird', 'the wing' will no longer be relative;

for if the so-called correlative is not winged, it follows that 'the wing' has no correlative.

Thus it is essential that the correlated terms should be exactly designated; if there is a name existing, the statement will be easy; if not, it is doubtless our duty to construct names. When the terminology is thus correct, it is evident that all correlatives are interdependent.

Correlatives are thought to come into existence simultaneously. This is for the most part true, as in the case of the double and the half. The existence of the half necessitates the existence of that of which it is a half. Similarly the existence of a master necessitates the existence of a slave, and that of a slave implies that of a master; these are merely instances of a general rule. Moreover, they cancel one another; for if there is no double it follows that there is no half, and vice versa; this rule also applies to all such correlatives. Yet it does not appear to be true in all cases that correlatives come into existence simultaneously. The object of knowledge would appear to exist before knowledge itself, for it is usually the case that we acquire knowledge of objects already existing; it would be difficult, if not impossible, to find a branch of knowledge the beginning of the existence of which was contemporaneous with that of its object.

Again, while the object of knowledge, if it ceases to exist, cancels at the same time the knowledge which was its correlative, the converse of this is not true. It is true that if the object of knowledge does not exist there can be no knowledge: for there will no longer be anything to know. Yet it is equally true that, if knowledge of a certain object does not exist, the object may nevertheless quite well exist. Thus, in the case of the squaring of the circle, if indeed that process is an object of knowledge, though it itself exists as an object of knowledge, yet the knowledge of it has not yet come into existence. Again, if all animals ceased to exist, there would be no knowledge, but there might yet be many objects of knowledge.

This is likewise the case with regard to perception: for the object of perception is, it appears, prior to the act of perception. If the perceptible is annihilated, perception also will cease to exist; but the annihilation of perception does not cancel the existence of the perceptible. For perception implies a body perceived and a body in which perception takes place. Now if that which is perceptible is annihilated, it follows that the body is annihilated, for the body is a perceptible thing; and if the body does not exist, it follows that perception also ceases to exist. Thus the annihilation of the perceptible involves that of perception.

But the annihilation of perception does not involve that of the perceptible. For if the animal is annihilated, it follows that perception also is annihilated, but perceptibles such as body, heat, sweetness, bitterness, and so on, will remain.

Again, perception is generated at the same time as the perceiving subject, for it comes into existence at the same time as the animal. But the perceptible surely exists before perception; for fire and water and such elements, out of which the animal is itself composed, exist before the animal is an animal at all, and before perception. Thus it would seem that the perceptible exists before perception.

It may be questioned whether it is true that no substance is relative, as seems to be the case, or whether exception is to be made in the case of certain secondary substances. With regard to primary substances, it is quite true that there is no such possibility, for neither wholes nor parts of primary substances are relative. The individual man or ox is not defined with reference to something external. Similarly with the parts: a particular hand or head is not defined as a particular hand or head of a particular person, but as the hand or head of a particular person. It is true also, for the most part at least, in the case of secondary substances; the species 'man' and the species 'ox' are not defined with reference to anything outside themselves. Wood, again, is only relative in so far as it is some one's property, not in so far as it is wood. It is plain, then, that in the cases mentioned substance is not relative. But with regard to some secondary substances there is a difference of opinion;

thus, such terms as 'head' and 'hand' are defined with reference to that of which the things indicated are a part, and so it comes about that these appear to have a relative character. Indeed, if our definition of that which is relative was complete, it is very difficult, if not impossible, to prove that no substance is relative. If, however, our definition was not complete, if those things only are properly called relative in the case of which relation to an external object is a necessary condition of existence, perhaps some explanation of the dilemma may be found.

The former definition does indeed apply to all relatives, but the fact that a thing is explained with reference to something else does not make it essentially relative.

From this it is plain that, if a man definitely apprehends a relative thing, he will also definitely apprehend that to which it is relative. Indeed this is self-evident: for if a man knows that some particular thing is relative, assuming that we call that a relative in the case of which relation to something is a necessary condition of existence, he knows that also to which it is related. For if he does not know at all that to which it is related, he will not know whether or not it is relative. This is clear, moreover, in particular instances. If a man knows definitely that such and such a thing is 'double', he will also forthwith know definitely that of which it is the double. For if there is nothing definite of which he knows it to be the double, he does not know at all that it is double. Again, if he knows that a thing is more beautiful, it follows necessarily that he will forthwith definitely know that also than which it is more beautiful. He will not merely know indefinitely that it is more beautiful than something which is less beautiful, for this would be supposition, not knowledge. For if he does not know definitely that than which it is more beautiful, he can no longer claim to know definitely that it is more beautiful than something else which is less beautiful: for it might be that nothing was less beautiful. It is, therefore, evident that if a man apprehends some relative thing definitely, he necessarily knows that also definitely to which it is related.

Now the head, the hand, and such things are substances, and it is possible to know their essential character definitely, but it does not necessarily follow that we should know that to which they are related. It is not possible to know forthwith whose head or hand is meant. Thus these are not relatives, and, this being the case, it would be true to say that no substance is relative in character. It is perhaps a difficult matter, in such cases, to make a positive statement without more exhaustive examination, but to have raised questions with regard to details is not without advantage.

8

By 'quality' I mean that in virtue of which people are said to be such and such.

Quality is a term that is used in many senses. One sort of quality let us call 'habit' or 'disposition'. Habit differs from disposition in being more lasting and more firmly established. The various kinds of knowledge and of virtue are habits, for knowledge, even when acquired only in a moderate degree, is, it is agreed, abiding in its character and difficult to displace, unless some great mental upheaval takes place, through disease or any such cause. The virtues, also, such as justice, self-restraint, and so on, are not easily dislodged or dismissed, so as to give place to vice.

By a disposition, on the other hand, we

mean a condition that is easily changed and quickly gives place to its opposite. Thus, heat, cold, disease, health, and so on are dispositions. For a man is disposed in one way or another with reference to these, but quickly changes, becoming cold instead of warm, ill instead of well. So it is with all other dispositions also, unless through lapse of time a disposition has itself become inveterate and almost impossible to dislodge: in which case we should perhaps go so far as to call it a habit.

It is evident that men incline to call those conditions habits which are of a more or less permanent type and difficult to displace; for those who are not retentive of knowledge, but volatile, are not said to have such and such a 'habit' as regards knowledge, yet they are disposed, we may say, either better or worse, towards knowledge. Thus habit differs from disposition in this, that while the latter in ephemeral, the former is permanent and difficult to alter.

Habits are at the same time dispositions, but dispositions are not necessarily habits. For those who have some specific habit may be said also, in virtue of that habit, to be thus or thus disposed; but those who are disposed in some specific way have not in all cases the corresponding habit.

Another sort of quality is that in virtue of which, for example, we call men good boxers or runners, or healthy or sickly: in fact it includes all those terms which refer to inborn capacity or incapacity. Such things are not predicated of a person in virtue of his disposition, but in virtue of his inborn capacity or incapacity to do something with ease or to avoid defeat of any kind. Persons are called good boxers or good runners, not in virtue of such and such a disposition, but in virtue of an inborn capacity to accomplish something with ease. Men are called healthy in virtue of the inborn capacity of easy resistance to those unhealthy influences that may ordinarily arise; unhealthy, in virtue of the lack of this capacity. Similarly with regard to softness and hardness. Hardness is predicated of a thing because it has that capacity of resistance which enables it to withstand disintegration; softness, again, is predicated of a thing by reason of the lack of that capacity.

A third class within this category is that of affective qualities and affections. Sweetness, bitterness, sourness, are examples of this sort of quality, together with all that is akin to these; heat, moreover, and cold, whiteness, and blackness are affective qualities. It is evident that these are qualities, for those things that possess them are themselves said to be such and such by reason of their presence. Honey is called sweet because it contains sweetness; the body is called white because it contains whiteness; and so in all other cases.

The term 'affective quality' is not used as indicating that those things which admit these qualities are affected in any way. Honey is not called sweet because it is affected in a specific way, nor is this what is meant in any other instance. Similarly heat and cold are called affective qualities, not because those things which admit them are affected. What is meant is that these said qualities are capable of producing an 'affection' in the way of perception. For sweetness has the power of affecting the sense of taste; heat, that of touch; and so it is with the rest of these qualities.

Whiteness and blackness, however, and the other colours, are not said to be affective qualities in this sense, but — because they themselves are the results of an affection. It is plain that many changes of colour take place because of affections. When a man is ashamed, he blushes; when he is afraid, he becomes pale, and so on. So true is this, that when a man is by nature liable to such affections, arising from some concomitance of elements in his constitution, it is a probable inference that he has the corresponding complexion of skin. For the same disposition of bodily elements, which in the former instance was momentarily present in the case of an access of shame, might be a result of a man's natural temperament, so as to produce the corresponding colouring also as a natural characteristic. All conditions, therefore, of this kind, if caused by certain permanent and lasting affections, are called affective qualities. For pallor and duskiness of complexion are called qualities, inasmuch as we are said to be such and such in virtue of them, not only if they originate in natural constitution, but also if they come about through long disease or sunburn, and are difficult to remove, or indeed remain throughout life. For in the same way we are said to be such and such because of these.

Those conditions, however, which arise from causes which may easily be rendered ineffective or speedily removed, are called, not qualities, but affections: for we are not said to be such virtue of them. The man who blushes through shame is not said to be a constitutional blusher, nor is the man who becomes pale through fear said to be constitutionally pale. He is said rather to have been affected.

Thus such conditions are called affections, not qualities.

In like manner there are affective qualities and affections of the soul. That temper with which a man is born and which has its origin in certain deep-seated affections is called a quality. I mean such conditions as insanity, irascibility, and so on: for people are said to be mad or irascible in virtue of these. Similarly those abnormal psychic states which are not inborn, but arise from the concomitance of certain other elements, and are difficult to remove, or altogether permanent, are called qualities, for in virtue of them men are said to be such and such.

Those, however, which arise from causes easily rendered ineffective are called affections, not qualities. Suppose that a man is irritable when vexed: he is not even spoken of as a bad-tempered man, when in such circumstances he loses his temper somewhat, but rather is said to be affected. Such conditions are therefore termed, not qualities, but affections.

The fourth sort of quality is figure and the shape that belongs to a thing; and besides this, straightness and curvedness and any other qualities of this type; each of these defines a thing as being such and such. Because it is triangular or quadrangular a thing is said to have a specific character, or again because it is straight or curved; in fact a thing's shape in every case gives rise to a qualification of it.

Rarity and density, roughness and smoothness, seem to be terms indicating quality: yet these, it would appear, really belong to a class different from that of quality. For it is rather a certain relative position of the parts composing the thing thus qualified which, it appears, is indicated by each of these terms. A thing is dense, owing to the fact that its parts are closely combined with one another; rare, because there are interstices between the parts; smooth, because its parts lie, so to speak, evenly; rough, because some parts project beyond others.

There may be other sorts of quality, but those that are most properly so called have, we may safely say, been enumerated.

These, then, are qualities, and the things that take their name from them as derivatives, or are in some other way dependent on them, are said to be qualified in some specific way. In most, indeed in almost all cases, the name of that which is qualified is derived from that of the quality. Thus the terms 'whiteness', 'grammar', 'justice', give us the adjectives 'white', 'grammatical', 'just', and so on.

There are some cases, however, in which, as the quality under consideration has no name, it is impossible that those possessed of it should have a name that is derivative. For instance, the name given to the runner or boxer, who is so called in virtue of an inborn capacity, is not derived from that of any quality; for lob those capacities have no name assigned to them. In this, the inborn capacity is distinct from the science, with reference to which men are called, e.g. boxers or wrestlers. Such a science is classed as a disposition; it has a name, and is called 'boxing' or 'wrestling' as the case may be, and the name given to those disposed in this way is derived from that of the science. Sometimes, even though a name exists for the quality, that which takes its character from the quality has a name that is not a derivative. For instance, the upright man takes his character from the possession of the quality of integrity, but the name given him is not derived from the word 'integrity'. Yet this does not occur often.

We may therefore state that those things are said to be possessed of some specific quality which have a name derived from that of the aforesaid quality, or which are in some other way dependent on it.

One quality may be the contrary of another; thus justice is the contrary of injustice, whiteness of blackness, and so on. The things, also, which are said to be such and such in virtue of these qualities, may be contrary the one to the other; for that which is unjust is contrary to that which is just, that which is white to that which is black. This, however, is not always the case. Red, yellow, and such colours, though qualities, have no contraries.

If one of two contraries is a quality, the other will also be a quality. This will be evident from particular instances, if we apply the names used to denote the other categories; for instance, granted that justice is the contrary of injustice and justice is a quality, injustice will also be a quality: neither quantity, nor relation, nor place, nor indeed any other category but that of quality, will be applicable properly to injustice. So it is with all other contraries falling under the category of quality.

Qualities admit of variation of degree. Whiteness is predicated of one thing in a greater or less degree than of another. This is also the case with reference to justice. Moreover, one and the same thing may exhibit a quality in a greater degree than it did before: if a thing is white, it may become whiter.

Though this is generally the case, there are exceptions. For if we should say that justice admitted of variation of degree, difficulties might ensue, and this is true with regard to all those qualities which are dispositions. There are some, indeed, who dispute the possibility of variation here. They maintain that justice and health cannot very well admit of variation of degree themselves, but that people vary in the degree in which they possess these qualities, and that this is the case with grammatical learning and all those qualities which are classed as dispositions. However that may be, it is an incontrovertible fact that the things which in virtue of these qualities are said to be what they are vary in the degree in which they possess them; for one man is said to be better versed in grammar, or more healthy or just, than another, and so on.

The qualities expressed by the terms 'triangular' and 'quadrangular' do not appear to admit of variation of degree, nor indeed do any that have to do with figure. For those things to which the definition of the triangle or circle is applicable are all equally triangular or circular. Those, on the other hand, to which the same definition is not applicable, cannot be said to differ from one another in degree; the square is no more a circle than the rectangle, for to neither is the definition of the circle appropriate. In short, if the definition of the term proposed is not applicable to both objects, they cannot be compared. Thus it is not all qualities which admit of variation of degree.

Whereas none of the characteristics I have mentioned are peculiar to quality, the fact that likeness and unlikeness can be predicated with reference to quality only, gives to that category its distinctive feature. One thing is like another only with reference to that in virtue of which it is such and such; thus this forms the peculiar mark of quality.

We must not be disturbed because it may be argued that, though proposing to discuss the category of quality, we have included in it many relative terms. We did say that habits and dispositions were relative. In practically all such cases the genus is relative, the individual not. Thus knowledge, as a genus, is explained by reference to something else, for we mean a knowledge of something. But particular branches of knowledge are not thus explained. The knowledge of grammar is not relative to anything external, nor is the knowledge of music, but these, if relative at all, are relative only in virtue of their genera; thus grammar is said be the knowledge of something, not the grammar of something; similarly music is the knowledge of something, not the music of something.

Thus individual branches of knowledge are not relative. And it is because we possess these individual branches of knowledge that we are said to be such and such. It is these that we actually possess: we are called experts because we possess knowledge in some particular branch. Those particular branches, therefore, of knowledge, in virtue of which we are sometimes said to be such and such, are themselves qualities, and are not relative. Further, if anything should happen to fall within both the category of quality and that of relation, there would be nothing extraordinary in classing it under both these heads.

9

Action and affection both admit of contraries and also of variation of degree. Heating is the contrary of cooling, being heated of being cooled, being glad of being vexed. Thus they admit of contraries. They also admit of variation of degree: for it is possible to heat in a greater or less degree; also to be heated in a greater or less degree. Thus action and affection also admit of variation of degree. So much, then, is stated with regard to these categories.

We spoke, moreover, of the category of position when we were dealing with that of relation, and stated that such terms derived their names from those of the corresponding attitudes.

As for the rest, time, place, state, since they are easily intelligible, I say no more about them than was said at the beginning, that in the category of state are included such states as 'shod', 'armed', in that of place 'in the Lyceum' and so on, as was explained before.

10

The proposed categories have, then, been adequately dealt with.

We must next explain the various senses in which the term 'opposite' is used. Things are said to be opposed in four senses: (i) as correlatives to one another, (ii) as contraries to one another, (iii) as privatives to positives, (iv) as affirmatives to negatives.

Let me sketch my meaning in outline. An instance of the use of the word 'opposite' with reference to correlatives is afforded by the expressions 'double' and 'half'; with reference to contraries by 'bad' and 'good'. Opposites in the sense of 'privatives' and 'positives' are' blindness' and 'sight'; in the sense of affirmatives and negatives, the propositions 'he sits', 'he does not sit'.

(i) Pairs of opposites which fall under the category of relation are explained by a reference of the one to the other, the reference being indicated by the preposition 'of' or by some other preposition. Thus, double is a relative term, for that which is double is explained as the double of something. Knowledge, again, is the opposite of the thing known, in the same sense; and the thing known also is explained by its relation to its opposite, knowledge. For the thing known is explained as that which is known by something, that is, by knowledge. Such things, then, as are opposite the one to the other in the sense of being correlatives are explained by a reference of the one to the other.

(ii) Pairs of opposites which are contraries are not in any way interdependent, but are contrary the one to the other. The good is not spoken of as the good of the bad, but as the contrary of the bad, nor is white spoken of as the white of the black, but as the contrary of the black. These two types of opposition are therefore distinct. Those contraries which are such that the subjects in which they are naturally present, or of which they are predicated, must necessarily contain either the one or the other of them, have no intermediate, but those in the case of which no such necessity obtains, always have an intermediate. Thus disease and health are naturally present in the body of an animal, and it is necessary that either the one or the other should be present in the body of an animal. Odd and even, again, are predicated of number, and it is necessary that the one or the other should be present in numbers. Now there is no intermediate between the terms of either of these two pairs. On the other hand, in those contraries with regard to which no such necessity obtains, we find an intermediate. Blackness and whiteness are naturally present in the body, but it is not necessary that either the one or the other should be present in the body, inasmuch as it is not true to say that everybody must be white or black. Badness and goodness, again, are predicated of man, and of many other things, but it is not necessary that either the one quality or the other should be present in that of which they are predicated: it is not true to say that everything that may be good or bad must be either good or bad. These pairs of contraries have intermediates: the intermediates between white and black are grey, sallow, and all the other colours that come between; the intermediate between good and bad is that which is neither the one nor the other.

Some intermediate qualities have names, such as grey and sallow and all the other colours that come between white and black; in other cases, however, it is not easy to name the intermediate, but we must define it as that which is not either extreme, as in the case of that which is neither good nor bad, neither just nor unjust.

(iii) 'privatives' and 'Positives' have reference to the same subject. Thus, sight and blindness have reference to the eye. It is a universal rule that each of a pair of opposites of this type has reference to that to which the particular 'positive' is natural. We say that that is capable of some particular faculty or possession has suffered privation when the faculty or possession in question is in no way present in that in which, and at the time at which, it should naturally be present. We do not call that toothless which has not teeth, or that blind which has not sight, but rather that which has not teeth or sight at the time when by nature it should. For there are some creatures which from birth are without sight, or without teeth, but these are not called toothless or blind.

To be without some faculty or to possess it is not the same as the corresponding 'privative' or 'positive'. 'Sight' is a 'positive', 'blindness' a 'privative', but 'to possess sight' is not equivalent to 'sight', 'to be blind' is not equivalent to 'blindness'. Blindness is a 'privative', to be blind is to be in a state of privation, but is not a 'privative'. Moreover, if 'blindness' were equivalent to 'being blind', both would be predicated of the same subject; but though a man is said to be blind, he is by no means said to be blindness.

To be in a state of 'possession' is, it appears, the opposite of being in a state of 'privation', just as 'positives' and 'privatives' themselves are opposite. There is the same type of antithesis in both cases; for just as blindness is opposed to sight, so is being blind opposed to having sight.

That which is affirmed or denied is not itself affirmation or denial. By 'affirmation' we mean an affirmative proposition, by 'denial' a negative. Now, those facts which form the matter of the affirmation or denial are not propositions; yet these two are said to be opposed in the same sense as the affirmation and denial, for in this case also the type of antithesis is the same. For as the affirmation is opposed to the denial, as in the two propositions 'he sits', 'he does not sit', so also the fact which constitutes the matter of the proposition in one case is opposed to that in the other, his sitting, that is to say, to his not sitting.

It is evident that 'positives' and 'privatives' are not opposed each to each in the same sense as relatives. The one is not explained by reference to the other; sight is not sight of blindness, nor is any other preposition used to indicate the relation. Similarly blindness is not said to be blindness of sight, but rather, privation of sight. Relatives, moreover, reciprocate; if blindness, therefore, were a relative, there would be a reciprocity of relation between it and that with which it was correlative. But this is not the case. Sight is not called the sight of blindness.

That those terms which fall under the heads of 'positives' and 'privatives' are not opposed each to each as contraries, either, is plain from the following facts: Of a pair of contraries such that they have no intermediate, one or the other must needs be present in the subject in which they naturally subsist, or of which they are predicated; for it is those, as we proved,' in the case of which this necessity obtains, that have no intermediate. Moreover, we cited health and disease, odd and even, as instances. But those contraries which have an intermediate are not subject to any such necessity. It is not necessary that every substance, receptive of such qualities, should be either black or white, cold or hot, for something intermediate between these contraries may very well be present in the subject. We proved, moreover, that those contraries have an intermediate in the case of which the said necessity does not obtain. Yet when one of the two contraries is a constitutive property of the subject, as it is a constitutive property of fire to be hot, of snow to be white, it is necessary determinately that one of the two contraries, not one or the other, should be present in the subject; for fire cannot be cold, or snow black. Thus, it is not the case here that one of the two must needs be present in every subject receptive of these qualities, but only in that subject of which the one forms a constitutive property. Moreover, in such cases it is one member of the pair determinately, and not either the one or the other, which must be present.

In the case of 'positives' and 'privatives', on the other hand, neither of the aforesaid statements holds good. For it is not necessary that a subject receptive of the qualities should always have either the one or the other; that which has not yet advanced to the state when sight is natural is not said either to be blind or to see. Thus 'positives' and 'privatives' do not belong to that class of contraries which consists of those which have no intermediate. On the other hand, they do not belong either to that class which consists of contraries which have an intermediate. For under certain conditions it is necessary that either the one or the other should form part of the constitution of every appropriate subject. For when a thing has reached the stage when it is by nature capable of sight, it will be said either to see or to be blind, and that in an indeterminate sense, signifying that the capacity may be either present or absent; for it is not necessary either that it should see or that it should be blind, but that it should be either in the one state or in the other. Yet in the case of those contraries which have an intermediate we found that it was never necessary that either the one or the other should be present in every appropriate subject, but only that in certain subjects one of the pair should be present, and that in a determinate sense. It is, therefore, plain that 'positives' and 'privatives' are not opposed each to each in either of the senses in which contraries are opposed.

Again, in the case of contraries, it is possible that there should be changes from either into the other, while the subject retains its identity, unless indeed one of the contraries is a constitutive property of that subject, as heat is of fire. For it is possible that that that which is healthy should become diseased, that which is white, black, that which is cold, hot, that which is good, bad, that which is bad, good. The bad man, if he is being brought into a better way of life and thought, may make some advance, however slight, and if he should once improve, even ever so little, it is plain that he might change completely, or at any rate make very great progress; for a man becomes more and more easily moved to virtue, however small the improvement was at first. It is, therefore, natural to suppose that he will make yet greater progress than he has made in the past; and as this process goes on, it will change him completely and establish him in the contrary state, provided he is not hindered by lack of time. In the case of 'positives' and 'privatives', however, change in both directions is impossible. There may be a change from possession to privation, but not from privation to possession. The man who has become blind does not regain his sight; the man who has become bald does not regain his hair; the man who has lost his teeth does not grow his grow a new set. (iv) Statements opposed as affirmation and negation belong manifestly to a class which is distinct, for in this case, and in this case only, it is necessary for the one opposite to be true and the other false.

Neither in the case of contraries, nor in the case of correlatives, nor in the case of 'positives' and 'privatives', is it necessary for one to be true and the other false. Health and disease are contraries: neither of them is true or false. 'Double' and 'half' are opposed to each other as correlatives: neither of them is true or false. The case is the same, of course, with regard to 'positives' and 'privatives' such as 'sight' and 'blindness'. In short, where there is no sort of combination of words, truth and falsity have no place, and all the opposites we have mentioned so far consist of simple words.

At the same time, when the words which enter into opposed statements are contraries, these, more than any other set of opposites, would seem to claim this characteristic. 'Socrates is ill' is the contrary of 'Socrates is well', but not even of such composite expressions is it true to say that one of the pair must always be true and the other false. For if Socrates exists, one will be true and the other false, but if he does not exist, both will be false; for neither 'Socrates is ill' nor 'Socrates is well' is true, if Socrates does not exist at all.

In the case of 'positives' and 'privatives', if the subject does not exist at all, neither proposition is true, but even if the subject exists, it is not always the fact that one is true and the other false. For 'Socrates has sight' is the opposite of 'Socrates is blind' in the sense of the word 'opposite' which applies to possession and privation. Now if Socrates exists, it is not necessary that one should be true and the other false, for when he is not yet able to acquire the power of vision, both are false, as also if Socrates is altogether non-existent.

But in the case of affirmation and negation, whether the subject exists or not, one is always false and the other true. For manifestly, if Socrates exists, one of the two propositions 'Socrates is ill', 'Socrates is not ill', is true, and the other false. This is likewise the case if he does not exist; for if he does not exist, to say that he is ill is false, to say that he is not ill is true. Thus it is in the case of those opposites only, which are opposite in the sense in which the term is used with reference to affirmation and negation, that the rule holds good, that one of the pair must be true and the other false.

11

That the contrary of a good is an evil is shown by induction: the contrary of health is disease, of courage, cowardice, and so on. But the contrary of an evil is sometimes a good, sometimes an evil. For defect, which is an evil, has excess for its contrary, this also being an evil, and the mean, which is a good, is equally the contrary of the one and of the other. It is only in a few cases, however, that we see instances of this: in most, the contrary of an evil is a good.

In the case of contraries, it is not always necessary that if one exists the other should also exist: for if all become healthy there will be health and no disease, and again, if everything turns white, there will be white, but no black. Again, since the fact that Socrates is ill is the contrary of the fact that Socrates is well, and two contrary conditions cannot both obtain in one and the same individual at the same time, both these contraries could not exist at once: for if that Socrates was well was a fact, then that Socrates was ill could not possibly be one.

It is plain that contrary attributes must needs be present in subjects which belong to the same species or genus. Disease and health require as their subject the body of an animal; white and black require a body, without further qualification; justice and injustice require as their subject the human soul.

Moreover, it is necessary that pairs of contraries should in all cases either belong to the same genus or belong to contrary genera or be themselves genera. White and black belong to the same genus, colour; justice and injustice, to contrary genera, virtue and vice; while good and evil do not belong to genera, but are themselves actual genera, with terms under them.

12

There are four senses in which one thing can be said to be 'prior' to another. Primarily and most properly the term has reference to time: in this sense the word is used to indicate that one thing is older or more ancient than another, for the expressions 'older' and 'more ancient' imply greater length of time.

Secondly, one thing is said to be 'prior' to another when the sequence of their being cannot be reversed. In this sense 'one' is 'prior' to 'two'. For if 'two' exists, it follows directly that 'one' must exist, but if 'one' exists, it does not follow necessarily that 'two' exists: thus the sequence subsisting cannot be reversed. It is agreed, then, that when the sequence of two things cannot be reversed, then that one on which the other depends is called 'prior' to that other.

In the third place, the term 'prior' is used with reference to any order, as in the case of science and of oratory. For in sciences which use demonstration there is that which is prior and that which is posterior in order; in geometry, the elements are prior to the propositions; in reading and writing, the letters of the alphabet are prior to the syllables. Similarly, in the case of speeches, the exordium is prior in order to the narrative.

Besides these senses of the word, there is a fourth. That which is better and more honourable is said to have a natural priority. In common parlance men speak of those whom they honour and love as 'coming first' with them. This sense of the word is perhaps the most far-fetched.

Such, then, are the different senses in which the term 'prior' is used.

Yet it would seem that besides those mentioned there is yet another. For in those things, the being of each of which implies that of the other, that which is in any way the cause may reasonably be said to be by nature 'prior' to the effect. It is plain that there are instances of this. The fact of the being of a man carries with it the truth of the proposition that he is, and the implication is reciprocal: for if a man is, the proposition wherein we allege that he is true, and conversely, if the proposition wherein we allege that he is true, then he is. The true proposition, however, is in no way the cause of the being of the man, but the fact of the man's being does seem somehow to be the cause of the truth of the proposition, for the truth or falsity of the proposition depends on the fact of the man's being or not being.

Thus the word 'prior' may be used in five senses.

13

The term 'simultaneous' is primarily and most appropriately applied to those things the genesis of the one of which is simultaneous with that of the other; for in such cases neither is prior or posterior to the other. Such things are said to be simultaneous in point of time. Those things, again, are 'simultaneous' in point of nature, the being of each of which involves that of the other, while at the same time neither is the cause of the other's being. This is the case with regard to the double and the half, for these are reciprocally dependent, since, if there is a double, there is also a half, and if there is a half, there is also a double, while at the same time neither is the cause of the being of the other.

Again, those species which are distinguished one from another and opposed one to another within the same genus are said to be 'simultaneous' in nature. I mean those species which are distinguished each from each by one and the same method of division. Thus the 'winged' species is simultaneous with the 'terrestrial' and the 'water' species. These are distinguished within the same genus, and are opposed each to each, for the genus 'animal' has the 'winged', the 'terrestrial', and the 'water' species, and no one of these is prior or posterior to another; on the contrary, all such things appear to be 'simultaneous' in nature. Each of these also, the terrestrial, the winged, and the water species, can be divided again into subspecies. Those species, then, also will be 'simultaneous' point of nature, which, belonging to the same genus, are distinguished each from each by one and the same method of differentiation.

But genera are prior to species, for the sequence of their being cannot be reversed. If there is the species 'water-animal', there will be the genus 'animal', but granted the being of the genus 'animal', it does not follow necessarily that there will be the species 'water-animal'.

Those things, therefore, are said to be 'simultaneous' in nature, the being of each of which involves that of the other, while at the same time neither is in any way the cause of the other's being; those species, also, which are distinguished each from each and opposed within the same genus. Those things, moreover, are 'simultaneous' in the unqualified sense of the word which come into being at the same time.

14

There are six sorts of movement: generation, destruction, increase, diminution, alteration, and change of place.

It is evident in all but one case that all these sorts of movement are distinct each from each. Generation is distinct from destruction, increase and change of place from diminution, and so on. But in the case of alteration it may be argued that the process necessarily implies one or other of the other five sorts of motion. This is not true, for we may say that all affections, or nearly all, produce in us an alteration which is distinct from all other sorts of motion, for that which is affected need not suffer either increase or diminution or any of the other sorts of motion. Thus alteration is a distinct sort of motion; for, if it were not, the thing altered would not only be altered, but would forthwith necessarily suffer increase or diminution or some one of the other sorts of motion in addition; which as a matter of fact is not the case. Similarly that which was undergoing the process of increase or was subject to some other sort of motion would, if alteration were not a distinct form of motion, necessarily be subject to alteration also. But there are some things which undergo increase but yet not alteration. The square, for instance, if a gnomon is applied to it, undergoes increase but not alteration, and so it is with all other figures of this sort. Alteration and increase, therefore, are distinct.

Speaking generally, rest is the contrary of motion. But the different forms of motion have their own contraries in other forms; thus destruction is the contrary of generation, diminution of increase, rest in a place, of change of place. As for this last, change in the reverse direction would seem to be most truly its contrary; thus motion upwards is the contrary of motion downwards and vice versa.

In the case of that sort of motion which yet remains, of those that have been enumerated, it is not easy to state what is its contrary. It appears to have no contrary, unless one should define the contrary here also either as 'rest in its quality' or as 'change in the direction of the contrary quality', just as we defined the contrary of change of place either as rest in a place or as change in the reverse direction. For a thing is altered when change of quality takes place; therefore either rest in its quality or change in the direction of the contrary may be called the contrary of this qualitative form of motion. In this way becoming white is the contrary of becoming black; there is alteration in the contrary direction, since a change of a qualitative nature takes place.

15

The term 'to have' is used in various senses. In the first place it is used with reference to habit or disposition or any other quality, for we are said to 'have' a piece of knowledge or a virtue. Then, again, it has reference to quantity, as, for instance, in the case of a man's height; for he is said to 'have' a height of three or four cubits. It is used, moreover, with regard to apparel, a man being said to 'have' a coat or tunic; or in respect of something which we have on a part of ourselves, as a ring on the hand: or in respect of something which is a part of us, as hand or foot. The term refers also to content, as in the case of a vessel and wheat, or of a jar and wine; a jar is said to 'have' wine, and a corn-measure wheat. The expression in such cases has reference to content. Or it refers to that which has been acquired; we are said to 'have' a house or a field. A man is also said to 'have' a wife, and a wife a husband, and this appears to be the most remote meaning of the term, for by the use of it we mean simply that the husband lives with the wife.

Other senses of the word might perhaps be found, but the most ordinary ones have all been enumerated.

ST. THOMAS AQUINAS - THE SUMMA THEOLOGICA

Whether, besides philosophy, any further doctrine is required?

Objection 1: It seems that, besides philosophical science, we have no need of any further knowledge. For man should not seek to know what is above reason: "Seek not the things that are too high for thee" (Ecclus. 3:22). But whatever is not above reason is fully treated of in philosophical science. Therefore any other knowledge besides philosophical science is superfluous.

Objection 2: Further, knowledge can be concerned only with being, for nothing can be known, save what is true; and all that is, is true. But everything that is, is treated of in philosophical science---even God Himself; so that there is a part of philosophy called theology, or the divine science, as Aristotle has proved (Metaph. vi). Therefore, besides philosophical science, there is no need of any further knowledge.

On the contrary, It is written (2 Tim. 3:16): "All Scripture, inspired of God is profitable to teach, to reprove, to correct, to instruct in justice." Now Scripture, inspired of God, is no part of philosophical science, which has been built up by human reason. Therefore it is useful that besides philosophical science, there should be other knowledge, i.e. inspired of God.

I answer that, It was necessary for

man's salvation that there should be a knowledge revealed by God besides philosophical science built up by human reason. Firstly, indeed, because man is directed to God, as to an end that surpasses the grasp of his reason: "The eye hath not seen, O God, besides Thee, what things Thou hast prepared for them that wait for Thee" (Is. 66:4). But the end must first be known by men who are to direct their thoughts and actions to the end. Hence it was necessary for the salvation of man that certain truths which exceed human reason should be made known to him by divine revelation. Even as regards those truths about God which human reason could have discovered, it was necessary that man should be taught by a divine revelation; because the truth about God such as reason could discover, would only be known by a few, and that after a long time, and with the admixture of many errors. Whereas man's whole salvation, which is in God, depends upon the knowledge of this truth. Therefore, in order that the salvation of men might be brought about more fitly and more surely, it was necessary that they should be taught divine truths by divine revelation. It was therefore necessary that besides philosophical science built up by reason, there should be a sacred science learned through revelation.

Reply to Objection 1: Although those things which are beyond man's knowledge may not be sought for by man through his reason, nevertheless, once they are revealed by God, they must be accepted by faith. Hence the sacred text continues, "For many things are shown to thee above the understanding of man" (Ecclus. 3:25). And in this, the sacred science consists.

Reply to Objection 2: Sciences are

differentiated according to the various means through which knowledge is obtained. For the astronomer and the physicist both may prove the same conclusion: that the earth, for instance, is round: the astronomer by means of mathematics (i.e. abstracting from matter), but the physicist by means of matter itself. Hence there is no reason why those things which may be learned from philosophical science, so far as they can be known by natural reason, may not also be taught us by another science so far as they fall within revelation. Hence theology included in sacred doctrine differs in kind from that theology which is part of philosophy.

Whether sacred doctrine is a science?

Objection 1: It seems that sacred

doctrine is not a science. For every science proceeds from self-evident principles. But sacred doctrine proceeds from articles of faith which are not self-evident, since their truth is not admitted by all: "For all men have not faith" (2 Thess. 3:2). Therefore sacred doctrine is not a science.

Objection 2: Further, no science deals with individual facts. But this sacred science treats of individual facts, such as the deeds of Abraham, Isaac and Jacob and such like. Therefore sacred doctrine is not a science.

On the contrary, Augustine says (De Trin. xiv, 1) "to this science alone belongs that whereby saving faith is begotten, nourished, protected and strengthened." But this can be said of no science except sacred doctrine. Therefore sacred doctrine is a science.

I answer that, Sacred doctrine is a science. We must bear in mind that there are two kinds of sciences. There are some which proceed from a principle known by the natural light of intelligence, such as arithmetic and geometry and the like. There are some which proceed from principles known by the light of a higher science: thus the science of perspective proceeds from principles established by geometry, and music from principles established by arithmetic. So it is that sacred doctrine is a science because it proceeds from principles established by the light of a higher science, namely, the science of God and the blessed. Hence, just as the musician accepts on authority the principles taught him by the mathematician, so sacred science is established on principles revealed by God.

Reply to Objection 1: The principles of any science are either in themselves self-evident, or reducible to the conclusions of a higher science; and such, as we have said, are the principles of sacred doctrine.

Reply to Objection 2: Individual facts are treated of in sacred doctrine, not because it is concerned with them principally, but they are introduced rather both as examples to be followed in our lives (as in moral sciences) and in order to establish the authority of those men through whom the divine revelation, on which this sacred scripture or doctrine is based, has come down to us.

Whether sacred doctrine is one science?

Objection 1: It seems that sacred doctrine is not one science; for according to the Philosopher (Poster. i) "that science is one which treats only of one class of subjects." But the creator and the creature, both of whom are treated of in sacred doctrine, cannot be grouped together under one class of subjects. Therefore sacred doctrine is not one science.

Objection   2: Further,   in   sacred doctrine we treat of angels, corporeal creatures and human morality. But these belong to separate philosophical sciences. Therefore sacred doctrine cannot be one science.

On the contrary, Holy Scripture speaks of it as one science: "Wisdom gave him the knowledge [scientiam] of holy things" (Wis. 10:10).

I answer that, Sacred doctrine is one science. The unity of a faculty or habit is to be gauged by its object, not indeed, in its material aspect, but as regards the precise formality under which it is an object. For example, man, ass, stone agree in the one precise formality of being colored; and color is the formal object of sight. Therefore, because Sacred Scripture considers things precisely under the formality of being divinely revealed, whatever has been divinely revealed possesses the one precise formality of the object of this science; and therefore is included under sacred doctrine as under one science.

Reply to Objection 1: Sacred doctrine does not treat of God and creatures equally, but of God primarily, and of creatures only so far as they are referable to God as their beginning or end. Hence the unity of this science is not impaired.

Reply to Objection 2: Nothing prevents inferior faculties or habits from being differentiated by something which falls under a higher faculty or habit as well; because the higher faculty or habit regards the object in its more universal formality, as the object of the "common sense" is whatever affects the senses, including, therefore, whatever is visible or audible. Hence the "common sense," although one faculty, extends to all the objects of the five senses. Similarly, objects which are the subject-matter of different philosophical sciences can yet be treated of by this one single sacred science under one aspect precisely so far as they can be included in revelation. So that in this way, sacred doctrine bears, as it were, the stamp of the divine science which is one and simple, yet extends to everything.

Whether sacred doctrine is a practical science?

Objection 1: It seems that sacred doctrine is a practical science; for a practical science is that which ends in action according to the Philosopher (Metaph. ii). But sacred doctrine is ordained to action: "Be ye doers of the word, and not hearers only" (James 1:22). Therefore sacred doctrine is a practical science.

Objection 2: Further, sacred doctrine is divided into the Old and the New Law. But law implies a moral science which is a practical science. Therefore sacred doctrine is a practical science.

On the contrary, Every practical science is concerned with human operations; as moral science is concerned with human acts, and architecture with buildings. But sacred doctrine is chiefly concerned with God, whose handiwork is especially man. Therefore it is not a practical but a speculative science.

I answer that, Sacred doctrine, being one, extends to things which belong to different philosophical sciences because it considers in each the same formal aspect, namely, so far as they can be known through divine revelation. Hence, although among the philosophical sciences one is speculative and another practical, nevertheless sacred doctrine includes both; as God, by one and the same science, knows both Himself and His works.

Still, it is speculative rather than practical because it is more concerned with divine things than with human acts; though it does treat even of these latter, inasmuch as man is ordained by them to the perfect knowledge of God in which consists eternal bliss. This is a sufficient answer to the Objections.

Whether sacred doctrine is nobler than other sciences?

Objection 1: It seems that sacred doctrine is not nobler than other sciences; for the nobility of a science depends on the certitude it establishes. But other sciences, the principles of which cannot be doubted, seem to be more certain than sacred doctrine; for its principles---namely, articles of faith---can be doubted. Therefore other sciences seem to be nobler.

Objection 2: Further, it is the sign of a lower science to depend upon a higher; as music depends on arithmetic. But sacred doctrine does in a sense depend upon philosophical sciences; for Jerome observes, in his Epistle to Magnus, that "the ancient doctors so enriched their books with the ideas and phrases of the philosophers, that thou knowest not what more to admire in them, their profane erudition or their scriptural learning." Therefore sacred doctrine is inferior to other sciences.

On the contrary, Other sciences are called the handmaidens of this one: "Wisdom sent her maids to invite to the tower" (Prov. 9:3).

I answer that, Since this science is partly speculative and partly practical, it transcends all others speculative and practical.

Now one speculative science is said to be nobler than another, either by reason of its greater certitude, or by reason of the higher worth of its subject-matter. In both these respects this science surpasses other speculative sciences; in point of greater certitude, because other sciences derive their certitude from the natural light of human reason, which can err; whereas this derives its certitude from the light of divine knowledge, which cannot be misled: in point of the higher worth of its subject-matter because this science treats chiefly of those things which by their sublimity transcend human reason; while other sciences consider only those things which are within reason's grasp. Of the practical sciences, that one is nobler which is ordained to a further purpose, as political science is nobler than military science; for the good of the army is directed to the good of the

State. But the purpose of this science, in so far as it is practical, is eternal bliss; to which as to an ultimate end the purposes of every practical science are directed. Hence it is clear that from every standpoint, it is nobler than other sciences.

Reply to Objection 1: It may well happen that what is in itself the more certain may seem to us the less certain on account of the weakness of our intelligence, "which is dazzled by the clearest objects of nature; as the owl is dazzled by the light of the sun" (Metaph. ii, lect. i). Hence the fact that some happen to doubt about articles of faith is not due to the uncertain nature of the truths, but to the weakness of human intelligence; yet the slenderest knowledge that may be obtained of the highest things is more desirable than the most certain knowledge obtained of lesser things, as is said in de Animalibus xi.

Reply to Objection 2: This science can in a sense depend upon the philosophical sciences, not as though it stood in need of them, but only in order to make its teaching clearer. For it accepts its principles not from other sciences, but immediately from God, by revelation. Therefore it does not depend upon other sciences as upon the higher, but makes use of them as of the lesser, and as handmaidens: even so the master sciences make use of the sciences that supply their materials, as political of military science. That it thus uses them is not due to its own defect or insufficiency, but to the defect of our intelligence, which is more easily led by what is known through natural reason (from which proceed the other sciences) to that which is above reason, such as are the teachings of this science.

Whether this doctrine is the same as

wisdom?

Objection 1: It seems that this doctrine is not the same as wisdom. For no doctrine which borrows its principles is worthy of the name of wisdom; seeing that the wise man directs, and is not directed (Metaph. i). But this doctrine borrows its principles. Therefore this science is not wisdom.

Objection 2: Further, it is a part of wisdom to prove the principles of other sciences. Hence it is called the chief of sciences, as is clear in Ethic. vi. But this doctrine does not prove the principles of other sciences. Therefore it is not the same as wisdom.

Objection 3: Further, this doctrine is acquired by study, whereas wisdom is acquired by God's inspiration; so that it is numbered among the gifts of the Holy Spirit (Is. 11:2). Therefore this doctrine is not the same as wisdom.

On the contrary, It is written (Dt. 4:6): "This is your wisdom and understanding in the sight of nations."

I answer that, This doctrine is wisdom above all human wisdom; not merely in any one order, but absolutely. For since it is the part of a wise man to arrange and to judge, and since lesser matters should be judged in the light of some higher principle, he is said to be wise in any one order who considers the highest principle in that order: thus in the order of building, he who plans the form of the house is called wise and architect, in opposition to the inferior laborers who trim the wood and make ready the stones: "As a wise architect, I have laid the foundation" (1 Cor. 3:10). Again, in the order of all human life, the prudent man is called wise, inasmuch as he directs his acts to a fitting end: "Wisdom is prudence to a man" (Prov. 10: 23).

Therefore he who considers absolutely the highest cause of the whole universe, namely God, is most of all called wise. Hence wisdom is said to be the knowledge of divine things, as Augustine says (De Trin. xii, 14). But sacred doctrine essentially treats of God viewed as the highest cause---not only so far as He can be known through creatures just as philosophers knew Him---"That which is known of God is manifest in them" (Rm. 1:19)---but also as far as He is known to Himself alone and revealed to others. Hence sacred doctrine is especially called wisdom.

Reply to Objection 1: Sacred doctrine derives its principles not from any human knowledge, but from the divine knowledge, through which, as through the highest wisdom, all our knowledge is set in order.

Reply to Objection 2: The principles of other sciences either are evident and cannot be proved, or are proved by natural reason through some other science. But the knowledge proper to this science comes through revelation and not through natural reason. Therefore it has no concern to prove the principles of other sciences, but only to judge of them. Whatsoever is found in other sciences contrary to any truth of this science must be condemned as false: "Destroying counsels and every height that exalteth itself against the knowledge of God" (2 Cor. 10:4,5).

Reply to Objection 3: Since judgment appertains to wisdom, the twofold manner of judging produces a twofold wisdom. A man may judge in one way by inclination, as whoever has the habit of a virtue judges rightly of what concerns that virtue by his very inclination towards it. Hence it is the virtuous man, as we read, who is the measure and rule of human acts. In another way, by knowledge, just as a man learned in moral science might be able to judge rightly about virtuous acts, though he had not the virtue. The first manner of judging divine things belongs to that wisdom which is set down among the gifts of the Holy Ghost: "The spiritual man judgeth all things" (1 Cor. 2:15). And Dionysius says (Div. Nom. ii): "Hierotheus is taught not by mere learning, but by experience of divine things." The second manner of judging belongs to this doctrine which is acquired by study, though its principles are obtained by revelation.

Whether God is the object of this science?

Objection 1: It seems that God is not the object of this science. For in every science, the nature of its object is presupposed. But this science cannot presuppose the essence of God, for Damascene says (De Fide Orth. i, iv): "It is impossible to define the essence of God."

Therefore God is not the object of this science.

Objection 2: Further, whatever conclusions are reached in any science must be comprehended under the object of the science. But in Holy Writ we reach conclusions not only concerning God, but concerning many other things, such as creatures and human morality. Therefore God is not the object of this science.

On the contrary, The object of the science is that of which it principally treats. But in this science, the treatment is mainly about God; for it is called theology, as treating of God. Therefore God is the object of this science.

I answer that, God is the object of this science. The relation between a science and its object is the same as that between a habit or faculty and its object. Now properly speaking, the object of a faculty or habit is the thing under the aspect of which all things are referred to that faculty or habit, as man and stone are referred to the faculty of sight in that they are colored. Hence colored things are the proper objects of sight. But in sacred science, all things are treated of under the aspect of God: either because they are God Himself or because they refer to God as their beginning and end. Hence it follows that God is in very truth the object of this science. This is clear also from the principles of this science, namely, the articles of faith, for faith is about God. The object of the principles and of the whole science must be the same, since the whole science is contained virtually in its principles. Some, however, looking to what is treated of in this science, and not to the aspect under which it is treated, have asserted the object of this science to be something other than God---that is, either things and signs; or the works of salvation; or the whole Christ, as the head and members. Of all these things, in truth, we treat in this science, but so far as they have reference to God.

Reply to Objection 1: Although we cannot know in what consists the essence of God, nevertheless in this science we make use of His effects, either of nature or of grace, in place of a definition, in regard to whatever is treated of in this science concerning God; even as in some philosophical sciences we demonstrate something about a cause from its effect, by taking the effect in place of a definition of the cause.

Reply to Objection 2: Whatever other conclusions are reached in this sacred science are comprehended under God, not as parts or species or accidents but as in some way related to Him.

Whether sacred doctrine is a matter of argument?

Objection 1: It seems this doctrine is not a matter of argument. For Ambrose says (De Fide 1): "Put arguments aside where faith is sought." But in this doctrine, faith especially is sought: "But these things are written that you may believe" (Jn. 20:31). Therefore sacred doctrine is not a matter of argument.

Objection 2: Further, if it is a matter of argument, the argument is either from authority or from reason. If it is from authority, it seems unbefitting its dignity, for the proof from authority is the weakest form of proof. But if it is from reason, this is unbefitting its end, because, according to Gregory (Hom. 26), "faith has no merit in those things of which human reason brings its own experience." Therefore sacred doctrine is not a matter of argument.

On the contrary, The Scripture says that a bishop should "embrace that faithful word which is according to doctrine, that he may be able to exhort in sound doctrine and to convince the gainsayers" (Titus 1:9).

I answer that, As other sciences do not argue in proof of their principles, but argue from their principles to demonstrate other truths in these sciences: so this doctrine does not argue in proof of its principles, which are the articles of faith, but from them it goes on to prove something else; as the Apostle from the resurrection of Christ argues in proof of the general resurrection (1 Cor. 15). However, it is to be borne in mind, in regard to the philosophical sciences, that the inferior sciences neither prove their principles nor dispute with those who deny them, but leave this to a higher science; whereas the highest of them, viz. metaphysics, can dispute with one who denies its principles, if only the opponent will make some concession; but if he concede nothing, it can have no dispute with him, though it can answer his objections. Hence Sacred Scripture, since it has no science above itself, can dispute with one who denies its principles only if the opponent admits some at least of the truths obtained through divine revelation; thus we can argue with heretics from texts in Holy Writ, and against those who deny one article of faith, we can argue from another. If our opponent believes nothing of divine revelation, there is no longer any means of proving the articles of faith by reasoning, but only of answering his objections---if he has any---against faith. Since faith rests upon infallible truth, and since the contrary of a truth can never be demonstrated, it is clear that the arguments brought against faith cannot be demonstrations, but are difficulties that can be answered.

Reply to Objection 1: Although arguments from human reason cannot avail to prove what must be received on faith, nevertheless, this doctrine argues from articles of faith to other truths.

Reply to Objection 2: This doctrine is especially based upon arguments from authority, inasmuch as its principles are obtained by revelation: thus we ought to believe on the authority of those to whom the revelation has been made. Nor does this take away from the dignity of this doctrine, for although the argument from authority based on human reason is the weakest, yet the argument from authority based on divine revelation is the strongest. But sacred doctrine makes use even of human reason, not, indeed, to prove faith (for thereby the merit of faith would come to an end), but to make clear other things that are put forward in this doctrine. Since therefore grace does not destroy nature but perfects it, natural reason should minister to faith as the natural bent of the will ministers to charity. Hence the Apostle says: "Bringing into captivity every understanding unto the obedience of Christ" (2 Cor. 10:5). Hence sacred doctrine makes use also of the authority of philosophers in those questions in which they were able to know the truth by natural reason, as Paul quotes a saying of Aratus: "As some also of your own poets said: For we are also His offspring" (Acts 17:28). Nevertheless, sacred doctrine makes use of these authorities as extrinsic and probable arguments; but properly uses the authority of the canonical Scriptures as an incontrovertible proof, and the authority of the doctors of the Church as one that may properly be used, yet merely as probable. For our faith rests upon the revelation made to the apostles and prophets who wrote the canonical books, and not on the revelations (if any such there are) made to other doctors. Hence Augustine says (Epis. ad Hieron. xix, 1): "Only those books of Scripture which are called canonical have I learned to hold in such honor as to believe their authors have not erred in any way in writing them. But other authors I so read as not to deem everything in their works to be true, merely on account of their having so thought and written, whatever may have been their holiness and learning."

Whether Holy Scripture should use metaphors?

Objection 1: It seems that Holy Scripture should not use metaphors. For that which is proper to the lowest science seems not to befit this science, which holds the highest place of all. But to proceed by the aid of various similitudes and figures is proper to poetry, the least of all the sciences. Therefore it is not fitting that this science should make use of such similitudes.

Objection 2: Further, this doctrine seems to be intended to make truth clear. Hence a reward is held out to those who manifest it: "They that explain me shall have life everlasting" (Ecclus. 24:31). But by such similitudes truth is obscured. Therefore, to put forward divine truths by likening them to corporeal things does not befit this science.

Objection 3: Further, the higher creatures are, the nearer they approach to the divine likeness. If therefore any creature be taken to represent God, this representation ought chiefly to be taken from the higher creatures, and not from the lower; yet this is often found in Scriptures.

On the contrary, It is written (Osee 12:10): "I have multiplied visions, and I have used similitudes by the ministry of the prophets." But to put forward anything by means of similitudes is to use metaphors. Therefore this sacred science may use metaphors.

I answer that, It is befitting Holy Writ to put forward divine and spiritual truths by means of comparisons with material things. For God provides for everything according to the capacity of its nature. Now it is natural to man to attain to intellectual truths through sensible objects, because all our knowledge originates from sense. Hence in Holy Writ, spiritual truths are fittingly taught under the likeness of material things. This is what Dionysius says (Coel. Hier. i): "We cannot be enlightened by the divine rays except they be hidden within the covering of many sacred veils." It is also befitting Holy Writ, which is proposed to all without distinction of persons---"To the wise and to the unwise I am a debtor" (Rm. 1:14)---that spiritual truths be expounded by means of figures taken from corporeal things, in order that thereby even the simple who are unable by themselves to grasp intellectual things may be able to understand it.

Reply to Objection 1: Poetry makes use of metaphors to produce a representation, for it is natural to man to be pleased with representations. But sacred doctrine makes use of metaphors as both necessary and useful.

Reply to Objection 2: The ray of divine revelation is not extinguished by the sensible imagery wherewith it is veiled, as Dionysius says (Coel. Hier. i); and its truth so far remains that it does not allow the minds of those to whom the revelation has been made, to rest in the metaphors, but raises them to the knowledge of truths; and through those to whom the revelation has been made others also may receive instruction in these matters. Hence those things that are taught metaphorically in one part of Scripture, in other parts are taught more openly. The very hiding of truth in figures is useful for the exercise of thoughtful minds and as a defense against the ridicule of the impious, according to the words "Give not that which is holy to dogs" (Mt. 7:6).

Reply to Objection 3: As Dionysius says, (Coel. Hier. i) it is more fitting that divine truths should be expounded under the figure of less noble than of nobler bodies, and this for three reasons. Firstly, because thereby men's minds are the better preserved from error. For then it is clear that these things are not literal descriptions of divine truths, which might have been open to doubt had they been expressed under the figure of nobler bodies, especially for those who could think of nothing nobler than bodies. Secondly, because this is more befitting the knowledge of God that we have in this life. For what He is not is clearer to us than what He is. Therefore similitudes drawn from things farthest away from God form within us a truer estimate that God is above whatsoever we may say or think of Him. Thirdly, because thereby divine truths are the better hidden from the unworthy.

Whether in Holy Scripture a word may have several senses?

Objection 1: It seems that in Holy Writ a word cannot have several senses, historical or literal, allegorical, tropological or moral, and anagogical. For many different senses in one text produce confusion and deception and destroy all force of argument. Hence no argument, but only fallacies, can be deduced from a multiplicity of propositions. But Holy Writ ought to be able to state the truth without any fallacy. Therefore in it there cannot be several senses to a word.

Objection 2: Further, Augustine says (De util. cred. iii) that "the Old Testament has a fourfold division as to history, etiology, analogy and allegory." Now these four seem altogether different from the four divisions mentioned in the first objection. Therefore it does not seem fitting to explain the same word of Holy Writ according to the four different senses mentioned above.

Objection 3: Further, besides these senses, there is the parabolical, which is not one of these four.

On the contrary, Gregory says (Moral. xx, 1): "Holy Writ by the manner of its speech transcends every science, because in one and the same sentence, while it describes a fact, it reveals a mystery."

I answer that, The author of Holy Writ is God, in whose power it is to signify His meaning, not by words only (as man also can do), but also by things themselves. So, whereas in every other science things are signified by words, this science has the property, that the things signified by the words have themselves also a signification. Therefore that first signification whereby words signify things belongs to the first sense, the historical or literal. That signification whereby things signified by words have themselves also a signification is called the spiritual sense, which is based on the literal, and presupposes it. Now this spiritual sense has a threefold division. For as the Apostle says (Heb. 10:1) the Old Law is a figure of the New Law, and Dionysius says (Coel. Hier. i) "the New Law itself is a figure of future glory." Again, in the New Law, whatever our Head has done is a type of what we ought to do. Therefore, so far as the things of the Old Law signify the things of the New Law, there is the allegorical sense; so far as the things done in Christ, or so far as the things which signify Christ, are types of what we ought to do, there is the moral sense. But so far as they signify what relates to eternal glory, there is the anagogical sense. Since the literal sense is that which the author intends, and since the author of Holy Writ is God, Who by one act comprehends all things by His intellect, it is not unfitting, as Augustine says (Confess. xii), if, even according to the literal sense, one word in Holy Writ should have several senses.

Reply to Objection 1: The multiplicity of these senses does not produce equivocation or any other kind of multiplicity, seeing that these senses are not multiplied because one word signifies several things, but because the things signified by the words can be themselves types of other things. Thus in Holy Writ no confusion results, for all the senses are founded on one---the literal---from which alone can any argument be drawn, and not from those intended in allegory, as Augustine says (Epis. 48). Nevertheless, nothing of Holy Scripture perishes on account of this, since nothing necessary to faith is contained under the spiritual sense which is not elsewhere put forward by the Scripture in its literal sense.

Reply to Objection 2: These three---history, etiology, analogy---are grouped under the literal sense. For it is called history, as Augustine expounds (Epis. 48), whenever anything is simply related; it is called etiology when its cause is assigned, as when Our Lord gave the reason why Moses allowed the putting away of wives---namely, on account of the hardness of men's hearts; it is called analogy whenever the truth of one text of Scripture is shown not to contradict the truth of another. Of these four, allegory alone stands for the three spiritual senses. Thus Hugh of St. Victor (Sacram. iv, 4 Prolog.) includes the anagogical under the allegorical sense, laying down three senses only---the historical, the allegorical, and the tropological.

Reply to Objection 3: The parabolical sense is contained in the literal, for by words things are signified properly and figuratively. Nor is the figure itself, but that which is figured, the literal sense. When Scripture speaks of God's arm, the literal sense is not that God has such a member, but only what is signified by this member, namely operative power. Hence it is plain that nothing false can ever underlie the literal sense of Holy Writ.

DESCARTES

Descartes' *Meditations*

MEDITATION I.
OF THE THINGS OF WHICH WE MAY DOUBT.

1. SEVERAL years have now elapsed since I first became aware that I had accepted, even from my youth, many false opinions for true, and that consequently what I afterward based on such principles was highly doubtful; and from that time I was convinced of the necessity of undertaking once in my life to rid myself of all the opinions I had adopted, and of commencing anew the work of building

from the foundation, if I desired to establish a firm and abiding superstructure in the sciences. But as this enterprise appeared to me to be one of great magnitude, I waited until I had attained an age so mature as to leave me no hope that at any stage of life more advanced I should be better able to execute my design. On this account, I have delayed so long that I should henceforth consider I was doing wrong were I still to consume in deliberation any of the time that now remains for action. To-day, then, since I have opportunely freed my mind from all cares [and am happily disturbed by no passions], and since I am in the secure possession of leisure in a peaceable retirement, I will at length apply myself earnestly and freely to the general overthrow of all my former opinions.

2. But, to this end, it will not be necessary for me to show that the whole of these are false--a

point, perhaps, which I shall never reach; but as even now my reason convinces me that I ought not the less carefully to withhold belief from what is not entirely certain and indubitable, than from what is manifestly false, it will be sufficient to justify the rejection of the whole if I shall find in each some ground for doubt. Nor for this purpose will it be necessary even to deal with each belief individually, which would be truly an endless labor; but, as the removal from below of the foundation necessarily involves the downfall of the whole edifice, I will at once approach the criticism of the principles on which all my former beliefs rested.

3. All that I have, up to this moment, accepted as possessed of the highest truth and certainty, I received either from or through the senses. I observed, however, that these sometimes misled us; and it is the part of

prudence not to place absolute confidence in that by which we have even once been deceived.

4. But it may be said, perhaps, that, although the senses occasionally mislead us respecting minute objects, and such as are so far removed from us as to be beyond the reach of close observation, there are yet many other of their informations (presentations), of the truth of which it is manifestly impossible to doubt; as for example, that I am in this place, seated by the fire, clothed in a winter dressing gown, that I hold in my hands this piece of paper, with other intimations of the same nature. But how could I deny that I possess these hands and this body, and withal escape being classed with persons in a state of insanity, whose brains are so disordered and clouded by dark bilious vapors as to cause them pertinaciously to assert that they are

monarchs when they are in the greatest poverty; or clothed [in gold] and purple when destitute of any covering; or that their head is made of clay, their body of glass, or that they are gourds? I should certainly be not less insane than they, were I to regulate my procedure according to examples so extravagant.

5. Though this be true, I must nevertheless here consider that I am a man, and that, consequently, I am in the habit of sleeping, and representing to myself in dreams those same things, or even sometimes others less probable, which the insane think are presented to them in their waking moments. How often have I dreamt that I was in these familiar circumstances, that I was dressed, and occupied this place by the fire, when I was lying undressed in bed? At the present moment, however, I certainly look upon this

paper with eyes wide awake; the head which I now move is not asleep; I extend this hand consciously and with express purpose, and I perceive it; the occurrences in sleep are not so distinct as all this. But I cannot forget that, at other times I have been deceived in sleep by similar illusions; and, attentively considering those cases, I perceive so clearly that there exist no certain marks by which the state of waking can ever be distinguished from sleep, that I feel greatly astonished; and in amazement I almost persuade myself that I am now dreaming.

6. Let us suppose, then, that we are dreaming, and that all these particulars--namely, the opening of the eyes, the motion of the head, the forth- putting of the hands--are merely illusions; and even that we really possess neither an entire body nor hands such as we see. Nevertheless it must be admitted at least

that the objects which appear to us in sleep are, as it were, painted representations which could not have been formed unless in the likeness of realities; and, therefore, that those general objects, at all events, namely, eyes, a head, hands, and an entire body, are not simply imaginary, but really existent. For, in truth, painters themselves, even when they study to represent sirens and satyrs by forms the most fantastic and extraordinary, cannot bestow upon them natures absolutely new, but can only make a certain medley of the members of different animals; or if they chance to imagine something so novel that nothing at all similar has ever been seen before, and such as is, therefore, purely fictitious and absolutely false, it is at least certain that the colors of which this is composed are real. And on the same principle, although these general objects, viz.

[a body], eyes, a head, hands, and the like, be imaginary, we are nevertheless absolutely necessitated to admit the reality at least of some other objects still more simple and universal than these, of which, just as of certain real colors, all those images of things, whether true and real, or false and fantastic, that are found in our consciousness *(cogitatio)*, are formed.

7. To this class of objects seem to belong corporeal nature in general and its extension; the figure of extended things, their quantity or magnitude, and their number, as also the place in, and the time during, which they exist, and other things of the same sort.

8. We will not, therefore, perhaps reason illegitimately if we conclude from this that Physics, Astronomy, Medicine, and all the

other sciences that have for their end the consideration of composite objects, are indeed of a doubtful character; but that Arithmetic, Geometry, and the other sciences of the same class, which regard merely the simplest and most general objects, and scarcely inquire whether or not these are really existent, contain somewhat that is certain and indubitable: for whether I am awake or dreaming, it remains true that two and three make five, and that a square has but four sides; nor does it seem possible that truths so apparent can ever fall under a suspicion of falsity [or incertitude].

9. Nevertheless, the belief that there is a God who is all powerful, and who created me, such as I am, has, for a long time, obtained steady possession of my mind. How, then, do I know that he has not arranged that there should be

neither earth, nor sky, nor any extended thing, nor figure, nor magnitude, nor place, providing at the same time, however, for [the rise in me of the perceptions of all these objects, and] the persuasion that these do not exist otherwise than as I perceive them ? And further, as I sometimes think that others are in error respecting matters of which they believe themselves to possess a perfect knowledge, how do I know that I am not also deceived each time I add together two and three, or number the sides of a square, or form some judgment still more simple, if more simple indeed can be imagined? But perhaps Deity has not been willing that I should be thus deceived, for he is said to be supremely good. If, however, it were repugnant to the goodness of Deity to have created me subject to constant deception, it would seem likewise to be contrary to his goodness to allow me to be occasionally deceived; and yet it is clear that this is permitted.

10. Some, indeed, might perhaps be found who would be disposed rather to deny the existence of a Being so powerful than to believe that there is nothing certain. But let us for the present refrain from opposing this opinion, and grant that all which is here said of a Deity is fabulous: nevertheless, in whatever way it be supposed that I reach the state in which I exist, whether by fate, or chance, or by an endless series of antecedents and consequents, or by any other means, it is clear (since to be deceived and to err is a certain defect) that the probability of my being so imperfect as to be the constant victim of deception, will be increased exactly in proportion as the power possessed by the

cause, to which they assign my origin, is lessened. To these reasonings I have assuredly nothing to reply, but am constrained at last to avow that there is nothing of all that I formerly believed to be true of which it is impossible to doubt, and that not through thoughtlessness or levity, but from cogent and maturely considered reasons; so that henceforward, if I desire to discover anything certain, I ought not the less carefully to refrain from assenting to those same opinions than to what might be shown to be manifestly false.

11. But it is not sufficient to have made these observations; care must be taken likewise to keep them in remembrance. For those old and customary opinions perpetually recur-- long and familiar usage giving them the right of occupying my mind, even almost against my will, and subduing my belief; nor will I lose

the habit of deferring to them and confiding in them so long as I shall consider them to be what in truth they are, viz, opinions to some extent doubtful, as I have already shown, but still highly probable, and such as it is much more reasonable to believe than deny. It is for this reason I am persuaded that I shall not be doing wrong, if, taking an opposite judgment of deliberate design, I become my own deceiver, by supposing, for a time, that all those opinions are entirely false and imaginary, until at length, having thus balanced my old by my new prejudices, my judgment shall no longer be turned aside by perverted usage from the path that may conduct to the perception of truth. For I am assured that, meanwhile, there will arise neither peril nor error from this course, and that I cannot for the present yield too much to distrust, since the end I now seek is not action but knowledge.

12. I will suppose, then, not that Deity, who is sovereignly good and the fountain of truth, but that some malignant demon, who is at once exceedingly potent and deceitful, has employed all his artifice to deceive me; I will suppose that the sky, the air, the earth, colors, figures, sounds, and all external things, are nothing better than the illusions of dreams, by means of which this being has laid snares for my credulity; I will consider myself as without hands, eyes, flesh, blood, or any of the senses, and as falsely believing that I am possessed of these; I will continue resolutely fixed in this belief, and if indeed by this means it be not in my power to arrive at the knowledge of truth, I shall at least do what is in my power, viz, [suspend my judgment], and guard with settled purpose against giving

my assent to what is false, and being imposed upon by this deceiver, whatever be his power and artifice. But this undertaking is arduous, and a certain indolence insensibly leads me back to my ordinary course of life; and just as the captive, who, perchance, was enjoying in his dreams an imaginary liberty, when he begins to suspect that it is but a vision, dreads awakening, and conspires with the agreeable illusions that the deception may be prolonged; so I, of my own accord, fall back into the train of my former beliefs, and fear to arouse myself from my

slumber, lest the time of laborious wakefulness that would succeed this quiet rest, in place of bringing any light of day, should prove inadequate to dispel the darkness that will arise from the difficulties that have now been raised.

PAXTON CASMIRO

SOCRATES - GLAUCON

I went down yesterday to the Piraeus with Glaucon the son of Ariston, that I might offer up my prayers to the goddess; and also because I wanted to see in what manner they would celebrate the festival, which was a new thing. I was delighted with the procession of the inhabitants; but that of the Thracians was equally, if not more, beautiful. When we had finished our prayers and viewed the spectacle, we turned in the direction of the city; and at that instant Polemarchus the son of Cephalus chanced to catch sight of us from a distance as we were starting on our way home, and toldhis servant to run and bid us wait for him. The servant took hold of me by the cloak behind, and said: Polemarchus desires you to wait.

I turned round, and asked him where his master was.
There he is, said the youth, coming after you, if you will only wait.

Certainly we will, said Glaucon; and in a few

minutes Polemarchus appeared, and with him Adeimantus, Glaucon's brother, Niceratus the son of Nicias, and several others who had been at the procession.

Socrates - POLEMARCHUS - GLAUCON - ADEIMANTUS

Polemarchus said to me: I perceive, Socrates, that you and our companion are already on your way to the city.

You are not far wrong, I said.
But do you see, he rejoined, how many we are?
Of course.
And are you stronger than all these? for if not, you will have to remain where you are.

May there not be the alternative, I said, that we may persuade you to let us go?

But can you persuade us, if we refuse to listen to you? he said.
Certainly not, replied Glaucon.
Then we are not going to listen; of that you

may be assured.

Adeimantus added: Has no one told you of the torch-race on horseback in honour of the goddess which will take place in the evening?

With horses! I replied: That is a novelty. Will horsemen carry torches and pass them one to another during the race?

Yes, said Polemarchus, and not only so, but a festival will he celebrated at night, which you certainly ought to see. Let us rise soon after supper and see this festival; there will be a gathering of young men, and we will have a good talk. Stay then, and do not be perverse.

Glaucon said: I suppose, since you insist, that we must.

Very good, I replied.

Glaucon - CEPHALUS - SOCRATES

Accordingly we went with Polemarchus to his house; and there we found his brothers Lysias and Euthydemus, and with them

Thrasymachus the Chalcedonian, Charmantides the Paeanian, and Cleitophon the son of Aristonymus. There too was Cephalus the father of Polemarchus, whom I had not seen for a long time, and I thought him very much aged. He was seated on a cushionedchair, and had a garland on his head, for he had been sacrificing in the court; and there were some other chairs in the room arranged in a semicircle, upon which we sat down by him. He saluted me eagerly, and then he said: --

You don't come to see me, Socrates, as often as you ought: If I were still able to go and see you I would not ask you to come to me. But at my age I can hardly get to the city, and therefore you should come oftener to the Piraeus. For let me tell you, that the more the pleasures of the body fade away, the greater to me is the pleasure and charm of conversation. Do not then deny my request, but make our house your resort and keep company with these young men; we are old friends, and you will be quite at home with us.

I replied: There is nothing which for my part I like better, Cephalus, than conversing with aged men; for I regard them as travellers who have gone a journey which I too may have to go, and of whom I ought to enquire, whether the way is smooth and easy, or rugged and difficult. And this is a question which I should like to ask of you who have arrived at that time which the poets call the 'threshold of old age' --Is life harder towards the end, or what report do you give of it?

I will tell you, Socrates, he said, what my own feeling is. Men of my age flock together; we are birds of a feather, as the old proverb says; and at our meetings the tale of my acquaintance commonly is --I cannot eat, I cannot drink; the pleasures of youth and love are fled away: there was a good time once, but now that is gone, and life is no longer life. Some complain of the slights which are put upon them by relations, and they will tell you sadly of how many evils their old age is the cause. But to me, Socrates, these complainers seem to blame that which is not really in fault. For if old age were the cause, I too being old, and every other old man, would have felt as they do. But this is not my own experience, nor that of others whom I have known. How well I remember the aged poet Sophocles, when in answer to the question, How does love suit with age, Sophocles, --are you still the man you were? Peace, he replied; most gladly have I escaped the thing of which you speak; I feel as if I had escaped from a mad and furious master. His words have often occurred to my mind since, and they seem as good to me now as at the time when he uttered them. For certainly old age has a great sense of calm and freedom; when the passions relax their hold, then, as Sophocles says, we are freed from the grasp not of one mad master only, but of many. The truth is, Socrates, that these regrets, and also the complaints about relations, are to be attributed to the same cause, which is not old age, but men's characters and tempers; for he who is of a calm and happy nature will hardly feel the pressure of age, but to him who is of an opposite disposition youth and age are equally a burden.

I listened in admiration, and wanting to draw
him out, that he might go on --Yes, Cephalus,
I said: but I rather suspect that people
in general are not convinced by you when you
speak thus; they think that old age sits lightly
upon you, not because of your happy
disposition, but because you are rich, and
wealth is well known to be a great comforter.

You are right, he replied; they are not
convinced: and there is something in what
they say; not, however, so much as they
imagine. I might answer them as Themistocles
answered the Seriphian who was abusing
him and saying that he was famous, not for his
own merits but because he was an Athenian: 'If
you had been a native of my country or I of
yours, neither of us would have been famous.'
And to those who are not rich and are
impatient of old age, the same reply may be
made; for to the good poor man old age cannot
be a light burden, nor can a bad rich man ever
have peace with himself.

May I ask, Cephalus, whether your fortune was for the most part inherited or acquired by you?

Acquired! Socrates; do you want to know how much I acquired? In the art of making money I have been midway between my father and grandfather: for my grandfather, whose name I bear, doubled and trebled the value of his patrimony, that which he inherited being much what I possess now; but my father Lysanias reduced the property below what it is at present: and I shall be satisfied if I leave to these my sons not less but a little more than I received.

That was why I asked you the question, I replied, because I see that you are indifferent about money, which is a characteristic rather of those who have inherited their fortunes than of those who have acquired them; the makers of fortunes have a second love of money as a creation of their own, resembling the affection of authors for their own poems, or of parents for their children, besides that natural love of it for the sake of use and profit which is common to them and all men. And hence they are very bad company, for they can talk about nothing but the praises of wealth. That is true, he said.

Yes, that is very true, but may I ask another question? What do you consider to be the greatest blessing which you have reaped from your wealth?

One, he said, of which I could not expect easily to convince others. For let me tell you, Socrates, that when a man thinks himself to be near death, fears and cares enter into his mind which he never had before; the tales of a world below and the punishment which is exacted there of deeds done here were once a laughing matter to him, but now he is tormented with the thought that they may be true: either from the weakness of age, or because he is now drawing nearer to that other place, he has a clearer view of these things; suspicions and alarms crowd thickly upon him, and he begins to reflect and consider what wrongs he has done to others. And when he finds that the sum of his transgressions is great he will many a time like a child start up in his sleep for fear, and he is filled with dark forebodings. But to him who is conscious of no sin, sweet hope, as Pindar charmingly says, is the kind nurse of his age:

Hope, he says, cherishes the soul of him who lives in justice and holiness and is the nurse of his age and the companion of his journey; -- hope which is mightiest to sway the restless soul of man.

How admirable are his words! And the great blessing of riches, I do not say to every man, but to a good man, is, that he has had no occasion to deceive or to defraud others, either intentionally or unintentionally; and when he departs to the world below he is not in any apprehension about offerings due to the gods or debts which he owes to men. Now to this peace of mind the possession of wealth greatly contributes; and therefore I say, that, setting one thing against another, of the many advantages which wealth has to give, to a man of sense this is in my opinion the greatest.

Well said, Cephalus, I replied; but as concerning justice, what is it? --to speak the truth and to pay your debts --no more than this? And even to this are there not exceptions? Suppose that a friend when in his right mind has deposited arms with me and he asks for them when he is not in his right mind, ought I to give them back to him? No one would say that I ought or that I should be right in doing so, any more than they would say that I ought always to speak the truth to one who is in his condition.

You are quite right, he replied.
But then, I said, speaking the truth and paying your debts is not a correct definition of justice.

Cephalus - SOCRATES - POLEMARCHUS

Quite correct, Socrates, if Simonides is to be

believed, said Polemarchus interposing.

I fear, said Cephalus, that I must go now, for I have to look after the sacrifices, and I hand over the argument to Polemarchus and the company.

Is not Polemarchus your heir? I said. To be sure, he answered, and went away laughing to the sacrifices.

Socrates - POLEMARCHUS

Tell me then, O thou heir of the argument, what did Simonides say, and according to you truly say, about justice?

He said that the repayment of a debt is just, and in saying so he appears to me to be right.

I should be sorry to doubt the word of such a wise and inspired man, but his meaning, though probably clear to you, is the reverse of clear to me. For he certainly does not mean, as we were now saying that I ought to return a return a deposit of arms or of anything else to one who asks for it when he is not in his right senses; and yet a deposit cannot be denied to be a debt.

True.
Then when the person who asks me is not in his right mind I am by no means to make the return?

Certainly not.
When Simonides said that the repayment of a debt was justice, he did not mean to include that case?

Certainly not; for he thinks that a friend ought always to do good to a friend and never evil.

You mean that the return of a deposit of gold which is to the injury of the receiver, if the two parties are friends, is not the repayment of a debt, --that is what you would imagine him to say?

Yes.

And are enemies also to receive what we owe to them?

To be sure, he said, they are to receive what we owe them, and an enemy, as I take it, owes to an enemy that which is due or proper to him -- that is to say, evil.

Simonides, then, after the manner of poets, would seem to have spoken darkly of the nature of justice; for he really meant to say that justice is the giving to each man what is proper to him, and this he termed a debt.

That must have been his meaning, he said.

By heaven! I replied; and if we asked him what due or proper thing is given by medicine, and to whom, what answer do you think that he would make to us?

He would surely reply that medicine gives drugs and meat and drink to human bodies.

And what due or proper thing is given by cookery, and to what?

Seasoning to food.

And what is that which justice gives, and to whom?

If, Socrates, we are to be guided at all by the analogy of the preceding instances, then justice is the art which gives good to friends and evil to enemies.

That is his meaning then?

I think so.

And who is best able to do good to his friends and evil to his enemies in time of sickness?

The physician.

Or when they are on a voyage, amid the perils of the sea?

The pilot.

And in what sort of actions or with a view to what result is the just man most able to do harm to his enemy and good to his friends?

In going to war against the one and in making alliances with the other.

But when a man is well, my dear Polemarchus, there is no need of a physician?

No.

And he who is not on a voyage has no need of a pilot?

No.

Then in time of peace justice will be of no use?

I am very far from thinking so.

You think that justice may be of use in peace as well as in war?

Yes.

Like husbandry for the acquisition of corn?

Yes.

Or like shoemaking for the acquisition of shoes, --that is what you mean?

Yes.

And what similar use or power of acquisition has justice in time of peace?

In contracts, Socrates, justice is of use.

And by contracts you mean partnerships?

Exactly.

But is the just man or the skilful player a more useful and better partner at a game of draughts?

The skilful player.
And in the laying of bricks and stones is the
just man a more useful or better partner than
the builder?

Quite the reverse.
Then in what sort of partnership is the just
man a better partner than the harp-player, as
in playing the harp the harp-player is certainly
a better partner than the just man?

In a money partnership.
Yes, Polemarchus, but surely not in the use of
money; for you do not want a just man to be
your counsellor the purchase or sale of a
horse; a man who is knowing about horses
would be better for that, would he not?

Certainly.
And when you want to buy a ship, the
shipwright or the pilot would be better?

True.
Then what is that joint use of silver or gold in

which the just man is to be preferred?

When you want a deposit to be kept safely.
You mean when money is not wanted, but
allowed to lie?
Precisely.
That is to say, justice is useful when money
is useless?
That is the inference.
And when you want to keep a pruning-hook
safe, then justice is useful to the individual and
to the state; but when you want to use it, then
the art of the vine-dresser?

Clearly.
And when you want to keep a shield or a lyre,
and not to use them, you would say that justice
is useful; but when you want to use them,
then the art of the soldier or of the musician?

Certainly.
And so of all the other things; --justice is
useful when they are useless, and useless when
they are useful?

That is the inference.

Then justice is not good for much. But let us consider this further point: Is not he who can best strike a blow in a boxing match or in any kind of fighting best able to ward off a blow?

Certainly.

And he who is most skilful in preventing or escaping from a disease is best able to create one?

True.

And he is the best guard of a camp who is best able to steal a march upon the enemy?

Certainly.

Then he who is a good keeper of anything is also a good thief?

That, I suppose, is to be inferred.

Then if the just man is good at keeping money, he is good at stealing it.

That is implied in the argument.

Then after all the just man has turned out to

be a thief. And this is a lesson which I suspect
you must have learnt out of Homer; for
he, speaking of Autolycus, the maternal
grandfather of Odysseus, who is a favourite of
his, affirms that

He was excellent above all men in theft and
perjury. And so, you and Homer and
Simonides are agreed that justice is an art of
theft; to be practised however 'for the good of
friends and for the harm of enemies,' --that
was what you were saying?

No, certainly not that, though I do not now
know what I did say; but I still stand by the
latter words.

Well, there is another question: By friends and
enemies do we mean those who are so really,
or only in seeming?

Surely, he said, a man may be expected to love
those whom he thinks good, and to hate those
whom he thinks evil.

Yes, but do not persons often err about good and evil: many who are not good seem to be so, and conversely?

That is true.
Then to them the good will be enemies and the evil will be their friends? True.

And in that case they will be right in doing good to the evil and evil to the good?

Clearly.
But the good are just and would not do an injustice?
True.
Then according to your argument it is just to injure those who do no wrong?

Nay, Socrates; the doctrine is immoral.
Then I suppose that we ought to do good to the just and harm to the unjust?

I like that better.
But see the consequence: --Many a man who is ignorant of human nature has friends who are

bad friends, and in that case he ought to do harm to them; and he has good enemies whom he ought to benefit; but, if so, we shall be saying the very opposite of that which we affirmed to be the meaning of Simonides.

Very true, he said: and I think that we had better correct an error into which we seem to have fallen in the use of the words 'friend' and 'enemy.'

What was the error, Polemarchus? I asked. We assumed that he is a friend who seems to be or who is thought good.

And how is the error to be corrected? We should rather say that he is a friend who is, as well as seems, good; and that he who seems only, and is not good, only seems to be and is not a friend; and of an enemy the same may be said.

You would argue that the good are our friends and the bad our enemies?

Yes.

And instead of saying simply as we did at first, that it is just to do good to our friends and harm to our enemies, we should further say: It is just to do good to our friends when they are good and harm to our enemies when they are evil?

Yes, that appears to me to be the truth.

But ought the just to injure any one at all?

Undoubtedly he ought to injure those who are both wicked and his enemies.

When horses are injured, are they improved or deteriorated?

The latter.

Deteriorated, that is to say, in the good qualities of horses, not of dogs?

Yes, of horses.

And dogs are deteriorated in the good qualities of dogs, and not of horses?

Of course.

And will not men who are injured be

deteriorated in that which is the proper virtue of man?

Certainly.
And that human virtue is justice?
To be sure.
Then men who are injured are of necessity made unjust?
That is the result.
But can the musician by his art make men unmusical?
Certainly not.
Or the horseman by his art make them bad horsemen?
Impossible.
And can the just by justice make men unjust, or speaking general can the good by virtue make them bad?

Assuredly not.
Any more than heat can produce cold?
It cannot.
Or drought moisture?
Clearly not.
Nor can the good harm any one?

Impossible.

And the just is the good?

Certainly.

Then to injure a friend or any one else is not
the act of a just man, but of the opposite, who
is the unjust?

I think that what you say is quite true,
Socrates.

Then if a man says that justice consists in the
repayment of debts, and that good is the debt
which a man owes to his friends, and evil
the debt which he owes to his enemies, --to say
this is not wise; for it is not true, if, as has been
clearly shown, the injuring of another can
be in no case just.

I agree with you, said Polemarchus.

Then you and I are prepared to take up arms
against any one who attributes such a saying to
Simonides or Bias or Pittacus, or any other
wise man or seer?

I am quite ready to do battle at your side,
he said.

Shall I tell you whose I believe the saying to
be?

Whose?

I believe that Periander or Perdiccas or Xerxes
or Ismenias the Theban, or some other rich
and mighty man, who had a great opinion of
his own power, was the first to say that justice
is 'doing good to your friends and harm to
your enemies.'

Most true, he said.

Yes, I said; but if this definition of justice also
breaks down, what other can be offered?

Several times in the course of the discussion
Thrasymachus had made an attempt to get the
argument into his own hands, and had been
put down by the rest of the company, who
wanted to hear the end. But when
Polemarchus and I had done speaking and
there was a pause, he could no longer hold his
peace; and, gathering himself up, he came at us
like a wild beast, seeking to devour us. We
were quite panic-stricken at the sight of him.

Socrates - POLEMARCHUS - THRASYMACHUS

He roared out to the whole company: What folly. Socrates, has taken possession of you all? And why, sillybillies, do you knock under to one another? I say that if you want really to know what justice is, you should not only ask but answer, and you should not seek honour to yourself from the refutation of an opponent, but have your own answer; for there is many a one who can ask and cannot answer. And now I will not have you say that justice is duty or advantage or profit or gain or interest, for this sort of nonsense will not do for me; I must have clearness and accuracy.

I was panic-stricken at his words, and could not look at him without trembling. Indeed I believe that if I had not fixed my eye upon him, I should have been struck dumb: but when I saw his fury rising, I looked at him first, and was therefore able to reply to him.

Thrasymachus, I said, with a quiver, don't be

hard upon us. Polemarchus and I may have been guilty of a little mistake in the argument, but I can assure you that the error was not intentional. If we were seeking for a piece of gold, you would not imagine that we were 'knocking under to one another,' and so losing our chance of finding it. And why, when we are seeking for justice, a thing more precious than many pieces of gold, do you say that we are weakly yielding to one another and not doing our utmost to get at the truth? Nay, my good friend, we are most willing and anxiousto do so, but the fact is that we cannot. And if so, you people who know all things should pity us and not be angry with us.

How characteristic of Socrates! he replied, with a bitter laugh; --that's your ironical style! Did I not foresee --have I not already told you, that whatever he was asked he would refuse to answer, and try irony or any other shuffle, in order that he might avoid answering?

You are a philosopher, Thrasymachus, I replied, and well know that if you ask a person what numbers make up twelve, taking care to prohibit him whom you ask from answering twice six, or three times four, or six times two, or four times three, 'for this sort of nonsense will not do for me,' --then obviously, that is your way of putting the question, no one can answer you. But suppose that he were to retort, 'Thrasymachus, what do you mean? If one of these numbers which you interdict be the true answer to the question, am I falsely to say some other number which is not the right one? --is that your meaning?' -How would you answer him?

Just as if the two cases were at all alike!
he said.
Why should they not be? I replied; and even if they are not, but only appear to be so to the person who is asked, ought he not to say what he thinks, whether you and I forbid him or not?

I presume then that you are going to make one of the interdicted answers?

I dare say that I may, notwithstanding the danger, if upon reflection I approve of any of them.

But what if I give you an answer about justice other and better, he said, than any of these? What do you deserve to have done to you?

Done to me! --as becomes the ignorant, I must learn from the wise --that is what I deserve to have done to me.

What, and no payment! a pleasant notion!
I will pay when I have the money, I replied.

Socrates - THRASYMACHUS - GLAUCON

But you have, Socrates, said Glaucon: and you, Thrasymachus, need be under no anxiety about money, for we will all make a contribution for Socrates.

Yes, he replied, and then Socrates will do as he always does --refuse to answer himself, but take and pull to pieces the answer of some one else.

Why, my good friend, I said, how can any one answer who knows, and says that he knows, just nothing; and who, even if he has some faint notions of his own, is told by a man of authority not to utter them? The natural thing is, that the speaker should be some one like yourself who professes to know and can tell what he knows. Will you then kindly answer, for the edification of the company and of myself?

Glaucon and the rest of the company joined in my request and Thrasymachus, as any one might see, was in reality eager to speak; for he thought that he had an excellent answer, and would distinguish himself. But at first he to insist on my answering; at length he consented to begin. Behold, he said, the wisdom of Socrates; he refuses to teach himself, and goes about learning of others, to whom he never even says thank you.

That I learn of others, I replied, is quite true;

but that I am ungrateful I wholly deny. Money I have none, and therefore I pay in praise, which is all I have: and how ready I am to praise any one who appears to me to speak well you will very soon find out when you answer; for I expect that you will answer well.

Listen, then, he said; I proclaim that justice is nothing else than the interest of the stronger. And now why do you not me? But of course you won't.

Let me first understand you, I replied. justice, as you say, is the interest of the stronger. What, Thrasymachus, is the meaning of this? You cannot mean to say that because Polydamas, the pancratiast, is stronger than we are, and finds the eating of beef conducive to his bodily strength, that to eat beef is therefore equally for our good who are weaker than he is, and right and just for us?

That's abominable of you, Socrates; you take the words in the sense which is most damaging to the argument.

Not at all, my good sir, I said; I am trying to understand them; and I wish that you would be a little clearer.

Well, he said, have you never heard that forms of government differ; there are tyrannies, and there are democracies, and there are aristocracies?

Yes, I know.
And the government is the ruling power in each state?
Certainly.
And the different forms of government make laws democratical, aristocratical, tyrannical, with a view to their several interests; and these laws, which are made by them for their own interests, are the justice which they deliver to their subjects, and him who transgresses them they punish as a breaker of the law, and unjust. And that is what I mean when I say that in all states there is the same principle of justice, which is the interest of the government; and as the government must be supposed to have

power, the only reasonable conclusion is, that everywhere there is one principle of justice, which is the interest of the stronger.

Now I understand you, I said; and whether you are right or not I will try to discover. But let me remark, that in defining justice you have yourself used the word 'interest' which you forbade me to use. It is true, however, that in your definition the words 'of the stronger' are added.

A small addition, you must allow, he said. Great or small, never mind about that: we must first enquire whether what you are saying is the truth. Now we are both agreed that justice is interest of some sort, but you go on to say 'of the stronger'; about this addition I am not so sure, and must therefore consider further.

Proceed.
I will; and first tell me, Do you admit that it is just or subjects to obey their rulers?

I do.
But are the rulers of states absolutely infallible, or are they sometimes liable to err?

To be sure, he replied, they are liable to err.
Then in making their laws they may sometimes make them rightly, and sometimes not?

True.
When they make them rightly, they make them agreeably to their interest; when they are mistaken, contrary to their interest; you admit that?

Yes.
And the laws which they make must be obeyed by their subjects, --and that is what you call justice?

Doubtless.
Then justice, according to your argument, is not only obedience to the interest of the stronger but the reverse?

What is that you are saying? he asked.

I am only repeating what you are saying, I believe. But let us consider: Have we not admitted that the rulers may be mistaken about their own interest in what they command, and also that to obey them is justice? Has not that been admitted?

Yes.

Then you must also have acknowledged justice not to be for the interest of the stronger, when the rulers unintentionally command things to be done which are to their own injury. For if, as you say, justice is the obedience which the subject renders to their commands, in that case, O wisest of men, is there any escape from the conclusion that the weaker are commanded to do, not what is for the interest, but what is for the injury of the stronger?

Nothing can be clearer, Socrates, said Polemarchus.

Socrates - CLEITOPHON - POLEMARCHUS - THRASYMACHUS

Yes, said Cleitophon, interposing, if you are allowed to be his witness.

But there is no need of any witness, said Polemarchus, for Thrasymachus himself acknowledges that rulers may sometimes command what is not for their own interest, and that for subjects to obey them is justice.

Yes, Polemarchus, --Thrasymachus said that for subjects to do what was commanded by their rulers is just.

Yes, Cleitophon, but he also said that justice is the interest of the stronger, and, while admitting both these propositions, he further acknowledged that the stronger may command the weaker who are his subjects to do what is not for his own interest; whence follows that justice is the injury quite as much as the interest of the stronger.

But, said Cleitophon, he meant by the interest of the stronger what the stronger thought to be his interest, --this was what the weaker had to do; and this was affirmed by him to be justice.

Those were not his words, rejoined Polemarchus.

Socrates - THRASYMACHUS

Never mind, I replied, if he now says that they are, let us accept his statement. Tell me, Thrasymachus, I said, did you mean by justice what the stronger thought to be his interest, whether really so or not?

Certainly not, he said. Do you suppose that I call him who is mistaken the stronger at the time when he is mistaken?

Yes, I said, my impression was that you did so, when you admitted that the ruler was not infallible but might be sometimes mistaken.

You argue like an informer, Socrates. Do you mean, for example, that he who is mistaken about the sick is a physician in that he is mistaken? or that he who errs in arithmetic or grammar is an arithmetician or grammarian at the me when he is making the mistake, in respect of the mistake? True, we say that the physician or arithmetician or grammarian has made a mistake, but this is only a way of speaking; for the fact is that neither the grammarian nor any other person of skill ever makes a mistake in so far as he is what his name implies; they none of them err unless their skill fails them, and then they cease to be skilled artists. No artist or sage or ruler errs at the time when he is what his name implies; though he is commonly said to err, and I adopted the common mode of speaking. But to be perfectly accurate, since you are such a lover of accuracy, we should say that the ruler, in so far as he is the ruler, is unerring, and, being unerring, always commands that which is for his own interest; and the subject is required to execute his commands; and therefore, as I said at first and now repeat, justice is the interest of the stronger.

Indeed, Thrasymachus, and do I really appear

to you to argue like an informer?

Certainly, he replied.
And you suppose that I ask these questions
with any design of injuring you in the
argument?

Nay, he replied, 'suppose' is not the word --I
know it; but you will be found out, and by
sheer force of argument you will never prevail.

I shall not make the attempt, my dear man; but
to avoid any misunderstanding occurring
between us in future, let me ask, in what sense
do you speak of a ruler or stronger whose
interest, as you were saying, he being
the superior, it is just that the inferior should
execute --is he a ruler in the popular or in the
strict sense of the term?

In the strictest of all senses, he said. And now
cheat and play the informer if you can; I ask no
quarter at your hands. But you never will be
able, never.

And do you imagine, I said, that I am such a madman as to try and cheat, Thrasymachus? I might as well shave a lion.

Why, he said, you made the attempt a minute ago, and you failed.
Enough, I said, of these civilities. It will be better that I should ask you a question: Is the physician, taken in that strict sense of which you are speaking, a healer of the sick or a maker of money? And remember that I am now speaking of the true physician.

A healer of the sick, he replied.
And the pilot --that is to say, the true pilot --is he a captain of sailors or a mere sailor?

A captain of sailors.
The circumstance that he sails in the ship is not to be taken into account; neither is he to be called a sailor; the name pilot by which he is distinguished has nothing to do with sailing, but is significant of his skill and of his authority over the sailors.

Very true, he said.

Now, I said, every art has an interest?

Certainly.

For which the art has to consider and provide?

Yes, that is the aim of art.

And the interest of any art is the perfection of it --this and nothing else?

What do you mean?

I mean what I may illustrate negatively by the example of the body. Suppose you were to ask me whether the body is self-sufficing or has wants, I should reply: Certainly the body has wants; for the body may be ill and require to be cured, and has therefore interests to which the art of medicine ministers; and this is the origin and intention of medicine, as you will acknowledge. Am I not right?

Quite right, he replied.

But is the art of medicine or any other art faulty or deficient in any quality in the same way that the eye may be deficient in sight or the ear fail of hearing, and therefore requires another art to provide for the interests of seeing and hearing --has art in itself, I say, any similar liability to fault or defect, and does every art require another supplementary art to provide for its interests, and that another and another without end? Or have the arts to look only after their own interests? Or have they no need either of themselves or of another? -- having no faults or defects, they have no need to correct them, either by the exercise of their own art or of any other; they have only to consider the interest of their subject-matter. For every art remains pure and faultless while remaining true --that is to say, while perfect and unimpaired. Take the words in your precise sense, and tell me whether I am not right."

Yes, clearly.
Then medicine does not consider the interest of medicine, but the interest of the body?

True, he said.
Nor does the art of horsemanship consider the interests of the art of horsemanship, but the interests of the horse; neither do any other

arts care for themselves, for they have no needs; they care only for that which is the subject of their art?

True, he said.
But surely, Thrasymachus, the arts are the superiors and rulers of their own subjects?

To this he assented with a good deal of reluctance.
Then, I said, no science or art considers or enjoins the interest of the stronger or superior, but only the interest of the subject and weaker?

He made an attempt to contest this proposition also, but finally acquiesced.

Then, I continued, no physician, in so far as he is a physician, considers his own good in what he prescribes, but the good of his patient; for the true physician is also a ruler having the human body as a subject, and is not a mere money-maker; that has been admitted?

Yes.

And the pilot likewise, in the strict sense of the term, is a ruler of sailors and not a mere sailor?

That has been admitted.

And such a pilot and ruler will provide and prescribe for the interest of the sailor who is under him, and not for his own or the ruler's interest?

He gave a reluctant 'Yes.'

Then, I said, Thrasymachus, there is no one in any rule who, in so far as he is a ruler, considers or enjoins what is for his own interest, but always what is for the interest of his subject or suitable to his art; to that he looks, and that alone he considers in everything which he says and does.

When we had got to this point in the argument, and every one saw that the definition of justice had been completely upset, Thrasymachus, instead of replying to me, said: Tell me, Socrates, have you got a nurse?

Why do you ask such a question, I said, when you ought rather to be answering?

Because she leaves you to snivel, and never wipes your nose: she has not even taught you to know the shepherd from the sheep.

What makes you say that? I replied.
Because you fancy that the shepherd or neatherd fattens of tends the sheep or oxen with a view to their own good and not to the good of himself or his master; and you further imagine that the rulers of states, if they are true rulers, never think of their subjects as sheep, and that they are not studying their own advantage day and night. Oh, no; and so entirely astray are you in your ideas about the just and unjust as not even to know that justice and the just are in reality another's good; that is to say, the interest of the ruler and stronger, and the loss of the subject and servant; and injustice the opposite; for the unjust is lord over the truly simple and just: he is the

stronger, and his subjects do what is for
his interest, and minister to his happiness,
which is very far from being their own.
Consider further, most foolish Socrates, that
the just is always a loser in comparison with
the unjust. First of all, in private
contracts: wherever the unjust is the partner of
the just you will find that, when the
partnership is dissolved, the unjust man has
always more and the just less. Secondly, in
their dealings with the State: when there is an
income tax, the just man will pay more and the
unjust less on the same amount of income; and
when there is anything to be received the one
gains nothing and the other much. Observe
also what happens when they take an
office;there is the just man neglecting his
affairs and perhaps suffering other losses, and
getting nothing out of the public, because he is
just; moreover he is hated by his friends and
acquaintance for refusing to serve them in
unlawful ways. But all this is reversed in the
case of the unjust man. I am speaking, as
before, of injustice on a large scale in which
the advantage of the unjust is more apparent;

and my meaning will be most clearly seen if we turn to that highest form of injustice in which the criminal is the happiest of men, and the sufferers or those who refuse to do injustice are the most miserable --that is to say tyranny, which by fraud and force takes away the property of others, not little by little but wholesale; comprehending in one, things sacred as well as profane, private and public; for which acts of wrong, if he were detected perpetrating any one of them singly, he would be punished and incur great disgrace --they who do such wrong in particular cases are called robbers of temples, and man-stealers and burglars and swindlers and thieves. But when a man besides taking away the money of the citizens has made slaves of them, then, instead of these names of reproach, he is termed happy and blessed, not only by the citizens but by all who hear of his having achieved the consummation of injustice. For mankind censure injustice, fearing that they may be the victims of it and not because they shrink from committing it. And thus, as I have shown, Socrates, injustice, when on a sufficient scale, has more strength and freedom and mastery than justice; and, as I said at first, justice is the interest of the stronger, whereas injustice is a man's own profit and interest.

Thrasymachus, when he had thus spoken, having, like a bathman, deluged our ears with his words, had a mind to go away. But the company would not let him; they insisted that he should remain and defend his position; and I myself added my own humble request that he would not leave us. Thrasymachus, I said to him, excellent man, how suggestive are your remarks! And are you going to run away before you have fairly taught or learned whether they are true or not? Is the attempt to determine the way of man's life so small a matter in your eyes --to determine how life may be passed by each one of us to the greatest advantage?

And do I differ from you, he said, as to the importance of the enquiry?

You appear rather, I replied, to have no care or thought about us, Thrasymachus --whether we live better or worse from not knowing what you say you know, is to you a matter of indifference. Prithee, friend, do not keep your knowledge to yourself; we are a large party; and any benefit which you confer upon us will be amply rewarded. For my own part I openly declare that I am not convinced, and that I do not believe injustice to be more gainful than justice, even if uncontrolled and allowed to have free play. For, granting that there may be an unjust man who is able tocommit injustice either by fraud or force, still this does not convince me of the superior advantage of injustice, and there may be others who are in the same predicament with myself. Perhaps we may be wrong; if so, you in your wisdom should convince us that we are mistaken in preferring justice to injustice.

And how am I to convince you, he said, if you are not already convinced by what I have just said; what more can I do for you? Would you have me put the proof bodily into your souls?

Heaven forbid! I said; I would only ask you to
be consistent; or, if you change, change openly
and let there be no deception. For I
must remark, Thrasymachus, if you will recall
what was previously said, that although you
began by defining the true physician in an
exact sense, you did not observe a like
exactness when speaking of the shepherd; you
thought that the shepherd as a shepherd tends
the sheep not with a view to their own good,
but like a mere diner or banqueter with a view
to the pleasures of the table; or, again, as a
trader for sale in the market, and not as a
shepherd. Yet surely the art of the shepherd is
concerned only with the good of his subjects;
he has only to provide the best for them, since
the perfection of the art is already ensured
whenever all the requirements of it are
satisfied. And that was what I was saying just
now about the ruler. I conceived that the art of
the ruler, considered as ruler, whether in a
state or in private life, could only regard the
good of his flock or subjects; whereas you seem
to think that the rulers in states, that is to say,

the true rulers, like being in authority.

Think! Nay, I am sure of it.
Then why in the case of lesser offices do men never take them willingly without payment, unless under the idea that they govern for the advantage not of themselves but of others? Let me ask you a question: Are not the several arts different, by reason of their each having a separate function? And, my dear illustrious friend, do say what you think, that we may make a little progress.

Yes, that is the difference, he replied.
And each art gives us a particular good and not merely a general one --medicine, for example, gives us health; navigation, safety at sea, and so on?

Yes, he said.
And the art of payment has the special function of giving pay: but we do not confuse this with other arts, any more than the art of the pilot is to be confused with the art of medicine, because the health of the pilot may

be improved by a sea voyage. You would not
be inclined to say, would you, that navigation
is the art of medicine, at least if we are to
adopt your exact use of language?

Certainly not.
Or because a man is in good health when he
receives pay you would not say that the art of
payment is medicine?

I should say not.
Nor would you say that medicine is the art of
receiving pay because a man takes fees when
he is engaged in healing?

Certainly not.
And we have admitted, I said, that the good of
each art is specially confined to the art?

Yes.
Then, if there be any good which all artists
have in common, that is to be attributed to
something of which they all have the
common use?

True, he replied.
And when the artist is benefited by receiving pay the advantage is gained by an additional use of the art of pay, which is not the art professed by him?

He gave a reluctant assent to this.
Then the pay is not derived by the several artists from their respective arts. But the truth is, that while the art of medicine gives health, and the art of the builder builds a house, another art attends them which is the art of pay. The various arts may be doing their own business and benefiting that over which they preside, but would the artist receive any benefit from his art unless he were paid as well?

I suppose not.
But does he therefore confer no benefit when he works for nothing?
Certainly, he confers a benefit.
Then now, Thrasymachus, there is no longer any doubt that neither arts nor governments provide for their own interests; but, as we were

before saying, they rule and provide for the interests of their subjects who are the weaker and not the stronger --to their good they attend and not to the good of the superior.

And this is the reason, my dear Thrasymachus, why, as I was just now saying, no one is willing to govern; because no one likes to take in hand the reformation of evils which are not his concern without remuneration. For, in the execution of his work, and in giving his orders to another, the true artist does not regard his own interest, but always that of his subjects; and therefore in order that rulers may be willing to rule, they must be paid in one of three modes of payment: money, or honour, or a penalty for refusing.

Socrates - GLAUCON

What do you mean, Socrates? said Glaucon. The first two modes of payment are intelligible enough, but what the penalty is I do not understand, or how a penalty can be a payment.

You mean that you do not understand the nature of this payment which to the best men is the great inducement to rule? Of course you know that ambition and avarice are held to be, as indeed they are, a disgrace?

Very true.

And for this reason, I said, money and honour have no attraction for them; good men do not wish to be openly demanding payment for governing and so to get the name of hirelings, nor by secretly helping themselves out of the public revenues to get the name of thieves. And not being ambitious they do not care about honour. Wherefore necessity must be laid upon them, and they must be induced to serve from the fear of punishment. And this, as I imagine, is the reason why the forwardness to take office, instead of waiting to be compelled, has been deemed dishonourable. Now the worst part of the punishment is that he who refuses to rule is liable to be ruled by one who is worse than himself. And the fear of this, as I conceive, induces the good to take office, not because they would, but because they cannot help --not under the idea that they are going to have any benefit or enjoyment themselves, but as a necessity, and because they are not able to commit the task of ruling to any one who is better than themselves, or indeed as good. For there is reason to think that if a city were composed entirely of good men, then to avoid office would be as much an object of contention as to obtain office is at present; then we should have plain proof that the true ruler is not meant by nature to regard his own interest, but that of his subjects; and every one who knew this would choose rather to receive a benefit from another than to have the trouble of conferring one. So far am I from agreeing with Thrasymachus that justice is the interest of the stronger. This latter question need not be further discussed at present; but when Thrasymachus says that the life of the unjust is more advantageous than that of the just, his new statement appears to me to be of a far more serious character. Which of us has spoken truly? And which sort of life, Glaucon, do you prefer?

I for my part deem the life of the just to be the more advantageous, he answered.

Did you hear all the advantages of the unjust which Thrasymachus was rehearsing?

Yes, I heard him, he replied, but he has not convinced me.
Then shall we try to find some way of convincing him, if we can, that he is saying what is not true?

Most certainly, he replied.
If, I said, he makes a set speech and we make another recounting all the advantages of being just, and he answers and we rejoin, there must be a numbering and measuring of the goods which are claimed on either side, and in the end we shall want judges to decide; but if we proceed in our enquiry as we lately did, by making admissions to one another, we shall unite the offices of judge and advocate in our own persons.

Very good, he said.

And which method do I understand you to prefer? I said.

That which you propose.

Well, then, Thrasymachus, I said, suppose you begin at the beginning and answer me. You say that perfect injustice is more gainful than perfect justice?

Socrates - GLAUCON - THRASYMACHUS

Yes, that is what I say, and I have given you my reasons.

And what is your view about them? Would you call one of them virtue and the other vice?

Certainly.

I suppose that you would call justice virtue and injustice vice?

What a charming notion! So likely too, seeing that I affirm injustice to be profitable and justice not.

What else then would you say?

The opposite, he replied.

And would you call justice vice?

No, I would rather say sublime simplicity.

Then would you call injustice malignity?

No; I would rather say discretion.

And do the unjust appear to you to be wise and good?

Yes, he said; at any rate those of them who are able to be perfectly unjust, and who have the power of subduing states and nations; but perhaps you imagine me to be talking of cutpurses.

Even this profession if undetected has advantages, though they are not to be compared with those of which I was just now speaking.

I do not think that I misapprehend your meaning, Thrasymachus, I replied; but still I cannot hear without amazement that you class injustice with wisdom and virtue, and justice with the opposite.

Certainly I do so class them.

Now, I said, you are on more substantial and almost unanswerable ground; for if the injustice which you were maintaining to be profitable had been admitted by you as by others to be vice and deformity, an answer might have been given to you on received principles; but now I perceive that you will call injustice honourable and strong, and to the unjust you will attribute all the qualities which were attributed by us before to the just, seeing that you do not hesitate to rank injustice with wisdom and virtue.

You have guessed most infallibly, he replied. Then I certainly ought not to shrink from going through with the argument so long as I have reason to think that you, Thrasymachus, are speaking your real mind; for I do believe that you are now in earnest and are not amusing yourself at our expense.

I may be in earnest or not, but what is that to you? --to refute the argument is your business.

Very true, I said; that is what I have to do: But
will you be so good as answer yet one more
question? Does the just man try to gain
any advantage over the just?

Far otherwise; if he did would not be the
simple, amusing creature which he is.

And would he try to go beyond just action?
He would not.
And how would he regard the attempt to gain
an advantage over the unjust; would that be
considered by him as just or unjust?

He would think it just, and would try to gain
the advantage; but he would not be able.

Whether he would or would not be able, I said,
is not to the point. My question is only
whether the just man, while refusing to have
more than another just man, would wish and
claim to have more than the unjust?

Yes, he would.
And what of the unjust --does he claim to have

more than the just man and to do more than is just

Of course, he said, for he claims to have more than all men.

And the unjust man will strive and struggle to obtain more than the unjust man or action, in order that he may have more than all?

True.

We may put the matter thus, I said --the just does not desire more than his like but more than his unlike, whereas the unjust desires more than both his like and his unlike?

Nothing, he said, can be better than that statement.

And the unjust is good and wise, and the just is neither?

Good again, he said.

And is not the unjust like the wise and good and the just unlike them?

Of course, he said, he who is of a certain nature, is like those who are of a certain nature; he who is not, not.

Each of them, I said, is such as his like is?
Certainly, he replied.
Very good, Thrasymachus, I said; and now to
take the case of the arts: you would admit that
one man is a musician and another not
a musician?

Yes.
And which is wise and which is foolish?
Clearly the musician is wise, and he who is not
a musician is foolish.

And he is good in as far as he is wise, and bad
in as far as he is foolish?

Yes.
And you would say the same sort of thing of
the physician?
Yes.
And do you think, my excellent friend, that a
musician when he adjusts the lyre would desire
or claim to exceed or go beyond a musician in
the tightening and loosening the strings?

I do not think that he would.

But he would claim to exceed the non-musician?

Of course.

And what would you say of the physician? In prescribing meats and drinks would he wish to go beyond another physician or beyond the practice of medicine?

He would not.

But he would wish to go beyond the non-physician?

Yes.

And about knowledge and ignorance in general; see whether you think that any man who has knowledge ever would wish to have the choice of saying or doing more than another man who has knowledge. Would he not rather say or do the same as his like in the same case?

That, I suppose, can hardly be denied.

And what of the ignorant? would he not desire to have more than either the knowing or the ignorant?

I dare say.
And the knowing is wise?
Yes.
And the wise is good?
True.
Then the wise and good will not desire to gain
more than his like, but more than his unlike
and opposite?

I suppose so.
Whereas the bad and ignorant will desire to
gain more than both?
Yes.
But did we not say, Thrasymachus, that the
unjust goes beyond both his like and unlike?
Were not these your words? They were.

They were.
And you also said that the lust will not go
beyond his like but his unlike?

Yes.
Then the just is like the wise and good, and the

unjust like the evil and ignorant?

That is the inference.
And each of them is such as his like is?
That was admitted.
Then the just has turned out to be wise and
good and the unjust evil and ignorant.

Thrasymachus made all these admissions, not
fluently, as I repeat them, but with extreme
reluctance; it was a hot summer's day, and the
perspiration poured from him in torrents; and
then I saw what I had never seen
before, Thrasymachus blushing. As we were
now agreed that justice was virtue
and wisdom, and injustice vice and ignorance,
I proceeded to another point:

Well, I said, Thrasymachus, that matter is now
settled; but were we not also saying that
injustice had strength; do you remember?

Yes, I remember, he said, but do not suppose
that I approve of what you are saying or have
no answer; if however I were to answer,

you would be quite certain to accuse me of haranguing; therefore either permit me to have my say out, or if you would rather ask, do so, and I will answer 'Very good,' as they say to story-telling old women, and will nod 'Yes' and 'No.'

Certainly not, I said, if contrary to your real opinion.

Yes, he said, I will, to please you, since you will not let me speak. What else would you have?

Nothing in the world, I said; and if you are so disposed I will ask and you shall answer.

Proceed.

Then I will repeat the question which I asked before, in order that our examination of the relative nature of justice and injustice may be carried on regularly. A statement was made that injustice is stronger and more powerful than justice, but now justice, having been identified with wisdom and virtue, is easily shown to be stronger than injustice, if injustice is ignorance; this can no longer be questioned by any one. But I want to view the matter, Thrasymachus, in a different way: You would not deny that a state may be unjust and may be unjustly attempting to enslave other states,or may have already enslaved them, and may be holding many of them in subjection?

True, he replied; and I will add the best and perfectly unjust state will be most likely to do so.

I know, I said, that such was your position; but what I would further consider is, whether this power which is possessed by the superior state can exist or be exercised without justice.

If you are right in you view, and justice is wisdom, then only with justice; but if I am right, then without justice.

I am delighted, Thrasymachus, to see you not only nodding assent and dissent, but making answers which are quite excellent.

That is out of civility to you, he replied.

You are very kind, I said; and would you have the goodness also to inform me, whether you think that a state, or an army, or a band of robbers and thieves, or any other gang of evil-doers could act at all if they injured one another?

No indeed, he said, they could not.
But if they abstained from injuring one another, then they might act together better?

Yes.
And this is because injustice creates divisions and hatreds and fighting, and justice imparts harmony and friendship; is not that true, Thrasymachus?

I agree, he said, because I do not wish to quarrel with you.
How good of you, I said; but I should like to know also whether injustice, having this tendency to arouse hatred, wherever existing, among slaves or among freemen, will not make them hate one another and set them at variance and render them incapable of

common action?

Certainly.
And even if injustice be found in two only, will they not quarrel and fight, and become enemies to one another and to the just

They will.
And suppose injustice abiding in a single person, would your wisdom say that she loses or that she retains her natural power?

Let us assume that she retains her power.
Yet is not the power which injustice exercises of such a nature that wherever she takes up her abode, whether in a city, in an army, in a family, or in any other body, that body is, to begin with, rendered incapable of united action by reason of sedition and distraction; and does it not become its own enemy and at variance with all that opposes it, and with the just? Is not this the case?

Yes, certainly.
And is not injustice equally fatal when existing

in a single person; in the first place rendering him incapable of action because he is not at unity with himself, and in the second place making him an enemy to himself and the just? Is not that true, Thrasymachus?

Yes.
And O my friend, I said, surely the gods are just?
Granted that they are.
But if so, the unjust will be the enemy of the gods, and the just will be their friend?

Feast away in triumph, and take your fill of the argument; I will not oppose you, lest I should displease the company.

Well then, proceed with your answers, and let me have the remainder of my repast. For we have already shown that the just are clearly wiser and better and abler than the unjust, and that the unjust are incapable of common action; nay ing at more, that to speak as we did of men who are evil acting at any time vigorously together, is not strictly true, for if they had been perfectly evil, they would have laid hands upon one another; but it is evident that there must have been some remnant of justice in them, which enabled them to combine; if there had not been they would haveinjured one another as well as their victims; they were but half --villains in their enterprises; for had they been whole villains, and utterly unjust, they would have been utterly incapable of action. That, as I believe, is the truth of the matter, and not what you said at first. But whether the just have a better and happier life than the unjust is a further question which we also proposed to consider. I think that they have, and for the reasons which to have given; but still I should like to examine further, for no light matter is at stake, nothing less than the rule of human life.

Proceed.
I will proceed by asking a question: Would you not say that a horse has some end?

I should.
And the end or use of a horse or of anything

would be that which could not be accomplished, or not so well accomplished, by any other thing?

I do not understand, he said.
Let me explain: Can you see, except with the eye?
Certainly not.
Or hear, except with the ear?
No.
These then may be truly said to be the ends of these organs?
They may.
But you can cut off a vine-branch with a dagger or with a chisel, and in many other ways?

Of course.
And yet not so well as with a pruning-hook made for the purpose?
True.
May we not say that this is the end of a pruning-hook?
We may.
Then now I think you will have no difficulty in

understanding my meaning when I asked the question whether the end of anything would be that which could not be accomplished, or not so well accomplished, by any other thing?

I understand your meaning, he said, and assent.

And that to which an end is appointed has also an excellence? Need I ask again whether the eye has an end?

It has.

And has not the eye an excellence?

Yes.

And the ear has an end and an excellence also?

True.

And the same is true of all other things; they have each of them an end and a special excellence?

That is so.

Well, and can the eyes fulfil their end if they are wanting in their own proper excellence and have a defect instead?

How can they, he said, if they are blind and cannot see?

You mean to say, if they have lost their proper excellence, which is sight; but I have not arrived at that point yet. I would rather ask the question more generally, and only enquire whether the things which fulfil their ends fulfil them by their own proper excellence, and fall of fulfilling them by their own defect?

Certainly, he replied.

I might say the same of the ears; when deprived of their own proper excellence they cannot fulfil their end?

True.

And the same observation will apply to all other things?

I agree.

Well; and has not the soul an end which nothing else can fulfil? for example, to superintend and command and deliberate and the like. Are not these functions proper to the soul, and can they rightly be assigned to any other?

To no other.
And is not life to be reckoned among the ends
of the soul?
Assuredly, he said.
And has not the soul an excellence also?
Yes.
And can she or can she not fulfil her own ends
when deprived of that excellence?

She cannot.
Then an evil soul must necessarily be an evil
ruler and superintendent, and the good soul a
good ruler?

Yes, necessarily.
And we have admitted that justice is the
excellence of the soul, and injustice the defect
of the soul?

That has been admitted.
Then the just soul and the just man will live
well, and the unjust man will live ill?

That is what your argument proves.

And he who lives well is blessed and happy,
and he who lives ill the reverse of happy?

Certainly.
Then the just is happy, and the unjust
miserable?
So be it.
But happiness and not misery is profitable.
Of course.
Then, my blessed Thrasymachus, injustice can
never be more profitable than justice.

Let this, Socrates, he said, be your
entertainment at the Bendidea.
For which I am indebted to you, I said, now
that you have grown gentle towards me and
have left off scolding. Nevertheless, I have not
been well entertained; but that was my own
fault and not yours. As an epicure snatches a
taste of every dish which is successively
brought to table, he not having allowed
himself time to enjoy the one before, so have I
gone from one subject to another without
having discovered what I sought at first, the
nature of justice. I left that enquiry and turned

away to consider whether justice is virtue and wisdom or evil and folly; and when there arose a further question about the comparative advantages of justice and injustice, I could not refrain from passing on to that. And the result of the whole discussion has been that I know nothing at all. For I know not what justice is, and therefore I am not likely to know whether it is or is not a virtue, nor can I say whether the just man is happy or unhappy.

Printed in Great Britain
by Amazon